W9-DGJ-729

DISCARD

Wheelchair **Warrior**

Wheelchair **Warrior**

GANGS, DISABILITY, AND BASKETBALL

Melvin Juette AND Ronald J. Berger

Temple University Press
Philadelphia

Temple University Press
1601 North Broad Street
Philadelphia PA 19122
www.temple.edu/tempress

Copyright © 2008 by Temple University
All rights reserved
Published 2008
Printed in the United States of America

Frontispiece: Copyright 2000 by Paralyzed Veterans of America,
by permission of *Sports 'N Spokes.* Mark Cowan, photographer.

Text design by Kate Nichols

∞ The paper used in this publication meets the requirements
of the American National Standard for Information Sciences—Permanence
of Paper for Printed Library Materials, ANSI Z39.48-1992

Library of Congress Cataloging-in-Publication Data

Juette, Melvin, 1969–
Wheelchair warrior : gangs, disability, and basketball /
Melvin Juette and Ronald J. Berger.
p.   cm.
Includes bibliographical references and index.
ISBN-13: 978-1-59213-474-8 (cloth : alk. paper)
ISBN-10: 1-59213-474-2 (cloth : alk. paper)
1. Juette, Melvin, 1969– 2. People with disabilities—United States—
Biography. 3. People with disabilities—Rehabilitation—United States.
4. Wheelchair basketball—United States. 5. Gang members—
United States—Biography. 6. Gang members—Rehabilitation—
United States. 7. Gangs—United States. I. Berger, Ronald J. II. Title.
HV3013.J84A3 2008
796.323'8—dc22
[B]
2007045406

2 4 6 8 9 7 5 3 1

Contents

Preface

Wheelchair Warrior tells the true story of Melvin Juette, an African American gang member from Chicago who was shot and paralyzed and later became a world-class wheelchair athlete. It is not primarily a story about urban black America, although it is also about that; rather, it is a story that focuses on Juette's resiliency in the face of his disability and how his involvement in wheelchair basketball helped him move forward with his life. Employing the life-story interview method, sociologist Ronald Berger assisted Juette in constructing a narrative that describes his quest, the personal and social hurdles he had to overcome, and the support he received from significant others along the way.

The book is intended to be read by a general audience as well as by students taking college courses on disability, sports, social problems, crime, and introductory sociology. It also will be of interest to scholars of the sociology of disability and sports, criminologists, life-story researchers, and professionals in the fields of therapeutic recreation and rehabilitative counseling. Berger's Introduction and Conclusion provide background material and analytical concepts that help illuminate Juette's life from a sociological perspective. But the body of the book, told in Juette's autobiographical voice, also can be read while bypassing these sections, as this compelling story can be appreciated on its own merits.

We thank Janet Francendese and the staff at Temple University Press for their support and guidance throughout the various stages of this project. We also thank Janet as well as Ruthy Berger, Lynne Rienner, and the reviewers of Temple University Press, especially Kent Sandstrom, for reading the manuscript and offering constructive suggestions. Finally, we express our appreciation to Sheila Juette, Brenda Martin, Mark Cowan, and Gregg Theune for their help with the selection and preparation of the photos, and to the following people who offered insights about the game of wheelchair basketball: Eric Barber, Amy Bleile, Tracy Chenowyth, Mike Frogley, Jeremy Lade, Richard Lee, Michael Lenser, and John Truesdale.

Introduction

Ronald J. Berger

D isability is a social enigma. Throughout history, people have felt compelled both to stare at the disabled in their midst and then turn their heads in discomfort. Franklin Roosevelt is considered by many to be one of the greatest presidents in the history of the United States, but he had to hide his polio-induced paralysis and use of a wheelchair lest the public think him too weak to lead the free world.[1] The Bible teaches that "Thou shalt not curse the deaf nor put a stumbling block before the blind" (*Leviticus*), but also that "If you do not carefully follow His commands and decrees . . . the Lord will afflict you with madness, blindness and confusion of mind" (*Deuteronomy*).[2]

The institution of the "freak show," which reached its heyday in the nineteenth century but lasted in the United States until the 1940s, featured the disabled as public spectacle. People with physical disabilities and bodily deformities, as well as tribal nonwhite "cannibals" and "savages," were displayed for public amusement and entertainment along with sword swallowers, snake charmers, bearded women, full-bodied tattooed people, and the like.[3]

The rise of the "medical model" of disability helped change this state of affairs. People with disabilities were now deemed worthy of medical diagnosis and treatment and viewed more benevolently.[4] But benevolence breeds pity, and the pitied are still stigmatized as less than full human beings. Thus, Jerry Lewis's annual muscular dystrophy telethon features pitiable "poster children" who help raise money for a preventive cure, but it does little to help improve the lives of those who are already disabled. Some may wonder why one would even want to live in such a state. The storyline of Clint Eastwood's 2004 Academy Award–winning *Million Dollar Baby* went so far as to suggest that euthanasia may be the most humane response to quadriplegia.[5]

In 2005, a film about disability of a radically different sort appeared on the cultural scene. Nominated for an Academy Award for best documentary, *Murderball* portrayed a group of wheelchair rugby players who challenged conventional views of disability. The highly competitive, outgoing, self-confident, and sexually active protagonists revealed an empowering side of the disability experience that relatively few people had seen. For readers of *Wheelchair Warrior,* it is our hope that the life story of Melvin Juette—the story of a gang member who was shot and paralyzed and became a world-class wheelchair basketball player—will do the same.

I first met Melvin when he was enrolled in my criminology course at the University of Wisconsin–Whitewater in the spring of 1990. He seemed a quiet youth at the time, unlike the vivacious man I later came to know. But, of course, like many students, he did not reveal much of himself to me. He would not have stood out among his classmates had he not been one of the relatively few black students at my university and one of even fewer black students in wheelchairs.

I became reacquainted with Melvin a few years later. Amy Bleile, another student who uses a wheelchair, was taking my criminology course. I had assigned the class an autobiography of a Los Angeles gang member to read.[6] Amy said she knew Melvin and told me that he had been a Chicago gang member who was shot and paralyzed in a gang dispute when he was sixteen years old. She suggested that I invite Melvin to speak to the class.

Melvin graciously agreed to be a guest speaker. It was then that I learned of his involvement in, indeed his passion for, wheelchair basketball. Later, he told me that he had always wanted to write a book about his life and the sport that he loved so much. Coincidence would have it that I also had an emerging interest in disability issues. My daughter had just been diagnosed with cerebral palsy, and I was seeking the counsel of those who had experience living with a disability. Thus, the personal and the professional merged for me as the project that led to this book began to unfold.

Melvin is a remarkable young man. His paralysis from the shooting, he often says, was "both the worst and best thing that happened" to him. If he had not been shot, he would have "probably ended up in prison or been killed, like so many of [his] former gang associates," friends and enemies alike. It was the reason he had gone on to college, made the U.S. national wheelchair basketball team, traveled throughout the world, and visited the White House for a photo op with the President of the United States.

Melvin had decided early on, when he was still recuperating in the hospital, that he was not "going to give in to self pity or despair." He remembered how he and his friends had reacted to James, a neighborhood youth with muscular dystrophy. "Although James used a power chair," Melvin recalls, "we all tried to include him in everything we did. We even changed the rules for touch football to accommodate him; if the passer hit James with the ball, it was counted as a catch. But James would at times feel sorry for himself, and some of the kids began to tire of his negative attitude" and stopped inviting him to play. Melvin didn't want "to end up like James." People told him he was in denial about his newly acquired disability, but he was determined to make the best of his situation.

People who write about disability often complain about the media's (and by inference my own) preoccupation with the so-called supercrips, those individuals whose inspirational stories of courage, dedication, and hard work prove that it can be done, that one can defy the odds and accomplish the impossible.[7] The concern is that these stories of success will foster unrealistic expectations about what people with disabilities can achieve, what they *should* be able to achieve, if only they tried hard enough. This myth of the "self-made man" implies that society does not need to change to accommodate the needs of people with disabilities.

I do not view Melvin as a supercrip, however. His story and the stories of others like him indicate that these individuals did not "make it" on their own.[8] These athletes—and indeed they are *athletes*—deserve credit for their perseverance and accomplishments in the face of adversity, but their lives must be understood in social context. Herein lies the crux of the sociological framework that informs this book: the dynamic interplay between *social structure* and *personal agency,* the two fundamental categories of general sociological discourse.[9]

Melvin's Life Story in Sociological Perspective

Sociologists use the concept of social structure to refer to patterns of social interaction and relationships that endure over time and that enable and/or constrain people's choices and opportunities. Social structure is, in a sense, external to individuals insofar as it is not of their own making and exists prior to their engagement with the world. Importantly, social structures are situated in time and place, in specific historical epochs and geographical environments.

Melvin grew up in Chicago in the 1970s and 1980s, on the city's south side, where the majority of residents are African American and many are poor. The South Side of Chicago is the city's largest section, covering over half of the metropolitan area. It includes commercial districts and spacious parks, as well as pleasant residential neighborhoods and poverty-stricken communities. For four decades, it was the location of Chicago's largest housing project, the infamous Robert Taylor Homes, where about 20,000 (mostly black) residents lived in twenty-eight crowded apartment complexes that spanned about fifteen city blocks. Before city officials decided to demolish the project in the early 2000s, it was infested with gangs, drugs, and crime.[10]

Melvin's parents were from an entirely different social milieu since they grew up in rural Mississippi. Although they were from stable and economically secure families, they sought greater opportunities in the North. They were part of a historic wave of rural-to-urban migration known as the Great Migration that increased the size of Chicago's African American population from 10 percent in 1910 to 40 percent by 1980.

The residential destination of African American migrants differed from those of whites who came from either the South or abroad. Local white residents resorted to a variety of exclusionary practices to segregate blacks—discriminatory neighborhood covenants and bank lending policies, vigilante violence, and white flight. Consequently, black newcomers tended to settle in racially homogeneous neighborhoods, and regardless of class status—the Juettes could be considered working or middle class—they were more likely than their white counterparts to live in or on the fringes of poor areas marked by high rates of crime and gang violence.[11]

Elijah Anderson, in his book *Code of the Street,* an ethnography of street life in Philadelphia, identified two residential value orientations, "decent" and "street," which African American residents used to describe their own neighbors. The so-called decent families, like the Juettes, are relatively better off financially than their street-oriented neighbors. They socialize their children to accept conventional values of hard work, self-reliance, respect for authority, religious faith, and self-improvement through education. They tend toward strict child-rearing practices and encourage their children to be on guard against troublesome peers.[12]

On the other hand, parents from so-called street families—who are more likely to be unmarried with children and lead lives complicated by drug or alcohol abuse or other self-destructive behaviors—socialize their children to accept the code of the street. In that code, receiving respect—being treated with proper deference—is highly regarded. Even a fleeting or awkward glance or eye contact that lingers too long can be taken as a sign of disrespect, or "dissing." Children witnessing interpersonal disputes learn, as Melvin did, that "might makes right." In almost every encounter, the victor is the one who physically wins the altercation, and this person enjoys the esteem and respect of onlookers. Humility or "turning the other cheek" is no virtue and can in fact be dangerous. Failure to respond to intimidation by others only encourages further violation.

Anderson observes that since youths from decent families go to school and hang out with kids from the street, the distinction between the two social types is not always clear. Thus, decent youths often adopt a street posture and learn to "code switch," that is, to behave according to different sets of rules in different situations. How far they will go in the direction of the street depends on how fully they have already been socialized by their parents, their degree of involvement in constructive social institutions, and their own decision making in the face of obstacles and opportunities that come their way.

Gangs are, of course, a prominent feature of the social environment confronted by urban youths. In large cities like Chicago, gangs have been around for decades. During the first half of the twentieth century, Chicago gang members were largely the children of economically disadvantaged European immigrants. By the time Melvin came of age, African American gangs, the history of which is described later in the book, had emerged as a dominant force on the streets. Regardless of historical era, youths have generally joined gangs for similar reasons: physical protection, fun and profit, and a sense of belonging to a close-knit group. Often, children have had older relatives, even parents and grandparents, who were involved in gangs. Moreover, gang members are not social outsiders in their communities; they are sons and daughters, grandchildren, nephews and nieces, and neighbors' kids. The majority of their time is not spent in law-violating activities, and they behave appropriately in most social situations.[13] Once Melvin got involved in gangs, for example, he still did well in school, attended church regularly, and even brought gang friends with him to Sunday services.

The core membership of a gang is generally tied to a particular neighborhood, or "hood." The city of Chicago, which expands over 228 square miles, has more than thirty identifiable neighborhoods. However, the notion of a neighborhood is somewhat of a misnomer since borders are permeable and disputed, and youths' networks of social relationships traverse these boundaries.[14] In Melvin's case, he joined a gang whose core membership was tied to a neighborhood outside of his area, which made him vulnerable to rival gangs within his own community.

The social-structural conditions that I have been describing do not, of course, exist independently of personal agency. They are ongoing accomplishments of people whose actions reproduce them in specific situational contexts. Nevertheless, people are not mere dupes or passive recipients of social structures; they are thinking, self-reflexive beings who are capable of assessing their circumstances, choosing among alternative courses of action, and consequently shaping their own behavior.[15] Through this capacity for personal agency, they exercise a degree of control over their lives and at times even manage to transform or reconfigure the social relationships in which they are enmeshed. Social psychologists often describe this as a matter of self-efficacy, that is, the ability to experience oneself as a causal agent capable of *acting on* rather than merely *reacting to* the external environment.[16] If this were not possible for people to do, personal and social change could not occur.

According to Mustaf Emirbayer and Ann Mische, personal agency consists of three interrelated yet analytically distinct components: the

habitual, projective, and practical-evaluative.[17] The *habitual* component entails social action that reproduces social structure; it is generally unreflective and taken for granted, although it is nonetheless
agentive since it entails attention, intention, and effort. Melvin, for
example, did not create the socially structured gang milieu in which
he found himself as a youth, but through his actions, he helped to
recreate or reproduce the conditions previously laid out for him.[18]

The *projective* component of agency entails the imaginative dimension of human consciousness, the ability to achieve cognitive
distance from the routine and envision future possibilities. Conflic-
tual or problematic situations are often the driving impetus for such
imaginative projection since they disrupt the taken-for-granted and
present themselves as challenges not easily resolved through habitual
modes of action. Norman Denzin calls these situations "epiphanies,"
moments of crisis or transformational experience that indelibly mark
people's lives.[19] Epiphanies have the power to "alter the fundamental
meaning structures" of life[20] and, as Arthur Frank observes, are therefore "privileged in their possibility" for personal growth and change.[21]
They can, on the other hand, also be potentially debilitating, occasions
of impotence and despair. In Melvin's case, his gunshot injury was the
epiphanic experience that compelled him to reflect on his life and seek
an alternative future. But in the initial phase of his recovery, it was not
clear to him what that future would entail. He found himself in what
Robert Murphy describes as a condition of "liminality," being betwixt
and between his life as an able-bodied and disabled-bodied person,
on the threshold of something new but not yet of it.[22]

Melvin's resolution of this dilemma relied on the third component
of agency highlighted in the scheme of Emirbayer and Mische—the
practical-evaluative, which consists of people's capacity to appraise
their options, mobilize personal and social resources, and engage in
adaptive, problem-solving actions. Practical-evaluative action draws
on past experience but applies or transposes it to new circumstances
in innovative ways. Until the shooting, for instance, Melvin had been

an accomplished member of the Chicago gang scene, someone who knew how to negotiate the streets. He was tough and agile, a capable fighter, a leader among peers, someone who commanded respect. Gang life had been a resource for constructing Melvin's sense of self-efficacy[23] as well as his masculine competence.[24] As a disabled man, however, Melvin now faced a world that often devalues men who lose control of their bodies, who appear vulnerable and weak, incomplete and inefficacious. For Melvin, wheelchair basketball was an alternative, practical resource for resolving his potentially debilitating and liminal status, retaining his sense of self-efficacy and manhood, and moving forward with his new life. The survival strategies he had learned on the streets of Chicago could be transposed to the basketball court. He could still be athletic, tough and competitive, resourceful and resolute, still experience his body as a masculine "presence," that is, as "an active power . . . which [could] be exercised on and over others."[25] At the same time, Melvin's new body opened the door to new ways of accomplishing masculine self-efficacy, as he became more empathetic, more considerate of others, a positive role model for youths in need.

Sociologists have long noted, to paraphrase Karl Marx, that people make their own history, but they do not do so under conditions of their choosing. As such, the possibilities for agentive or self-efficacious action in the face of disability are not entirely of one's own making. Successful life outcomes under such circumstances also require social-structural resources and opportunities. Thus, Melvin's successful adaptation to his spinal-cord injury must be understood in terms of the broader context of changing claims about disability that have been advanced by proponents of the contemporary disability rights movement. It is this movement that has been the progenitor of a powerful cultural shift in our understanding of disability, one that has provided Melvin and others like him with a narrative or "rhetoric of self-change," as Frank would put it, that has helped them move beyond stigma and pity.[26]

Building on the accomplishments of other "oppositional consciousness" movements of the 1960s and early 1970s,[27] the contemporary disability rights movement viewed disability as an institutionalized source of oppression comparable to inequalities based on race, gender, and sexual orientation. Critiquing the "medical model" of disability, which emphasized people's personal adjustment to impairment and their adaptation to a medical-rehabilitative regimen of treatment, disability rights activists advanced a "social model" of disability, claiming that it is not an individual's impairment but the socially imposed barriers—the inaccessible buildings, the limited modes of transportation and communication, the prejudicial attitudes—that constructed disability as a subordinate social status and devalued life experience.[28]

Advocates of disability rights also rejected conventional assumptions of the disabled as abnormal, inferior, or dependent people who at best should be pitied or treated as objects of charitable goodwill. While disability may never be wished for and is often a great source of suffering, people with disabilities differ quite dramatically in the nature of their impairment, and their condition is not always as "wholly disastrous" as some might imagine.[29] People with disabilities commonly learn to appreciate and enhance their remaining abilities and strive for goals and qualities of human worth that are still within their grasp.[30] Adapting the discourse of identity politics and multiculturalism that had been integral to other oppositional movements, people who shared a common experience of stigmatization and discrimination challenged societal ideals of normality and promoted disability as an acceptable, even celebrated, form of social difference.[31]

Identity politics as applied to disability has had its limitations, however. Many people who are disabled, Melvin included, do not identify themselves as such. They do not dismiss their impairment as irrelevant, but neither do they internalize its significance.[32] Moreover, "people with disabilities" is not a homogeneous category; it consists of individuals with varying needs and interests who "may have little in common except the stigma society imposes on them."[33] The divide between people with physical and cognitive impairments is but one example of the divisions. After Melvin was released from the hospital, for instance, school officials assigned him to a special high school that segregated students with disabilities. He was placed in classes with those who had severe cognitive disabilities, and he did not like being treated like someone who was mentally impaired. The "supercrip" complaint is another manifestation of the divisions within the disability community. It stems from a discord between those who want to play sports recreationally (or not at all) and those, like Melvin, who want to play competitively at the elite levels of the sport.

Disability, Sports, and Basketball

Sociologists view sports as a social institution through which cultural conceptions of "desirable and normalized" bodies are constructed.[34] At first it might seem obvious that the "disabled" body stands (or sits) in contradistinction to the "athletic" body. To some, the notion of a disabled athlete in a wheelchair may even seem to be an oxymoron, as people with mobility impairments are, for the most part, unable to participate in sports that have "historically been oriented to the able-bodied."[35] On the other hand, the experience of dedicated wheelchair athletes, like Melvin and the protagonists in *Murderball*, suggests another side of the story. These are individuals who have resisted stigmatized views of their physical capabilities by devoting themselves to athletic activities that allow them to embrace rather than reject their impairments. They are, in the terms of Michael Schwalbe and Douglas Mason-Schrock, engaged in a process of "oppositional identity work," transforming a potentially discrediting identity (i.e., disability) into a crediting one (i.e., athleticism) so that they may be seen as representing a "noble rather than flawed character."[36]

Sports for people with mobility impairments are a mid-twentieth century phenomenon, a by-product of World War II, when improved battlefield evacuation methods and medical technologies dramatically increased the survival rate of the wounded. These soldiers, including those with spinal-cord injuries, would have died in previous wars. Now they survived, warehoused in veterans hospitals throughout the United States. Many of these individuals previously enjoyed participation in competitive sports and would not tolerate inactivity. They started playing pool, table tennis, and catch, and then progressed to swimming and bowling, and eventually to water polo, softball, touch football, and basketball. Today, people with disabilities participate in the full gamut of sports, including bicycling, skiing, tennis, track and field, rugby, volleyball, and horseback riding.[37]

Among all the sports currently available for people with disabilities, wheelchair basketball is arguably the most popular. In the United States, the National Wheelchair Basketball Association (NWBA), organized in 1949, boasts a membership of more than 2,000 athletes. It organizes men's, women's, and youth divisions and sponsors more than 200 teams. Although the NWBA is an amateur organization, a number of its teams receive financial support from, and bear the names of, professional National Basketball Association teams. In addition, a United States national team competes every four years in the international Paralympics, which is held in the same venue as the regular Olympic Games, and in the Wheelchair Basketball World Championship, or Gold Cup, which is held every four years in the off years between the Paralympics.

Jay Coakley notes that the "performance ethic" of competitive sports entails several elements of what it means to be an "athlete": sacrificing other interests for "the game," striving for distinction, accepting the risk of defeat, playing through pain, and refusing to accept limits on the pursuit of excellence.[38] Sociologists of sports are often critical of this ethic because it sometimes devolves into a hyper-masculinity of sorts whereby athletes take performance-enhancing drugs and develop an attitude of hubris and a desire to humiliate or even physically harm an opponent during a game.[39] Indeed, some viewers of *Murderball* were critical of the masculinist ethic exuded by some of the players, who took great joy in a game that allowed them to "hit" and smash into their opponents. Thus, as competitive opportunities for playing wheelchair sports have expanded, critics have questioned whether people with disabilities actually benefit from emulating the athletic model.[40]

At the same time, it is also true that a person can derive much inner strength from a commitment to work hard to excel, to push oneself to the limit, to be as good as one can be. When someone is faced with the challenge of living with a disability, sports can be a resource that helps him or her move forward with a sense of determination. In fact, a large body of research indicates that participation in sports entails substantial benefits for people with disabilities.[41] For many, the primary benefit is the intrinsic satisfaction, the reward felt for playing the game, accomplishing the task itself. Others enjoy the camaraderie and affirmation that they get from teammates and peers. Participants gain improved physical conditioning and a sense of bodily mastery, along with a heightened sense of self-efficacy that spills over into other social pursuits. They learn to view "challenges as possibilities rather than as obstacles," to deal with defeat not as failure but as incentive to do better.[42] These enhancements are not simply "rehabilitative" or "therapeutic," for they are the same ones often enjoyed by the nondisabled who participate in athletics.

Even those who enjoy basketball may not appreciate the special skills involved in this sport if they have never seen a wheelchair game, especially a game played by elite athletes like Melvin. During my informal observations and conversations with spectators at games, I found people to be truly in awe of what they see. They are amazed that players can accurately shoot at a ten-foot-high basket from the three-point line, the free-throw line, or even closer, *while sitting in a chair*. They are enamored with how effortlessly the players maneuver their chairs with such speed and agility, maintaining their stamina for the duration of a forty- or forty-eight-minute game. And they are impressed with the players' durability as they witness the physical contact, chairs banging against chairs, chairs tipping over as players fall to the ground and then pull themselves up without assistance from others. During the course of a game, onlookers tend to forget that these are people with disabilities. Instead, they see incredible *athletes* doing things that an untrained, able-bodied person simply could not do. The players' bodies communicate a different meaning, tell a different story, that disrupts conventional assumptions about people with disabilities.

Methodology: Constructing the Life Story

Before beginning Melvin's story, a few observations about research method are in order so that we may situate our approach in "methodological context." *Wheelchair Warrior* participates in a time-honored tradition of social research that has "vacillated in acceptance and popularity over the years."[43] Variously called interpretive biography, life-history research, or life-story research, among other terms,[44] this qualitative genre aims to advance what C. Wright Mills famously called the "sociological imagination," a sociology that grapples with the intersection of biography and history in society and the ways in which personal troubles are related to public issues.[45] By documenting stories that reflect the interplay between personal agency and social structure, this method strives to recreate the "experiential integrity of human existence" as seen from the vantage point of those whose lives are being revealed.[46] By linking personal stories to collective narratives (e.g., the gang or disability experience), biographical accounts give voice to muted memories and allow society to "speak itself" through the lives of individuals.[47]

Some sociologists are concerned, however, that by acknowledging that every person has *his or her own story* to tell, biographical inquiry risks substituting commonsense accounts for sociological analyses. According to this view, it generally takes a trained observer to make sociological sense of the story. As Jaber Gubrium and James Holstein note, it is fine to allow "indigenous voices [to] have their own say," but researchers should not abandon their authorial obligation to "complement and contextualize the explication of [subjects'] accounts, or nonaccounts, as the case may be."[48] The challenge, of course, is to decide how to balance the *analytic* and *storied* components of the biography, to decide whether one or the other should be given privileged status in the narrative that is told, and to choose which should be foreground and which should be background.[49]

Carol Gill observes that much disability research has privileged analysis over story, whereby researchers' theoretical and methodological constructs have taken precedence over the conveyance of subjects' experiences.[50] In doing so, Gill argues, the individual and collective voices of the disabled have been silenced and marginalized. More generally, Ann Goetting views the biographical method as a remedy to this marginalization and is leery of researchers whose primary goal is to dissect or deconstruct life stories for the sake of the analytical enterprise.[51] Rather, sociologists should collect and tell stories to make connections with readers—to generate empathy, build social bonds, make it more difficult to dismiss others as irrelevant or inferior.[52] Although analytical understanding remains important, the stories that we tell should help readers locate and make sense of their own lives in light of the experience of others, to "aid each of us in our own transformation of unique experience into sociological text."[53]

Melvin and I gathered the data for the book as I guided him through several informal interview sessions that yielded more than twenty hours of tape-recorded material, which I transcribed verbatim. Melvin began by chronologically reconstructing his life through the best of his recollection and according to his own relevancies, animating his story with conversational exchanges and details of thought and action that imbued it with verisimilitude.[54] I occasionally intervened to ask Melvin questions and encourage him to elaborate with more detail, and in subsequent sessions, we focused on particular

topics, such as family and friends, gang culture, hospital rehabilitation, and wheelchair basketball.

In the writing of the book, Melvin and I made a conscious decision to keep his story intact, to write the main part of the book as an
autobiography, and to bracket the sociological analysis in the Introduction and Conclusion. Although I helped edit and fashion Melvin's
account into a coherent written narrative, I took great pains to do
so in a way that allowed Melvin to retain ownership of the story as
we continually exchanged multiple drafts through various stages of
revision until we arrived at the final manuscript. On the other hand,
we did take some minor license with the life-story method in the
strictest sense, as we decided to include brief historical accounts of
Chicago gangs and the game of wheelchair basketball to give readers
greater appreciation of the social context in which Melvin's life was
embedded. (We felt this was especially important for those readers
who might choose to bypass the Introduction and Conclusion, as we
noted in the Preface.) I assisted Melvin in researching these sections
by sharing material from published sources that added a little detail
to the knowledge he had acquired through personal experience. We
also culled back issues of *Sports 'N Spokes* magazine for details regarding games he played in, and we talked to several individuals from the
University of Wisconsin–Whitewater basketball community—John
Truesdale, Mike Frogley, Eric Barber, and Jeremy Lade—who contributed some details that enhanced their part in Melvin's story.

Storytelling is, of course, an ancient human endeavor, and the
telling of a life story necessarily involves appropriation of
general narrative formats and archetypical experiences that structure
how people tell and write about their lives.[55] Thus, our story about
Melvin's life relies (implicitly and explicitly) on conventional plot-
making devices: It has a beginning, middle, and end and is marked
by key turning points or epiphanies in which the protagonist (Melvin) exercises agency in the face of adversity, falters and progresses,

and ultimately triumphs. It also adopts what Frank refers to as the archetypal "quest" narrative. According to Frank, the quest narrative reframes adversity—and in the case of an illness or acquired disability, an "interruption" of a life—as a challenge that hinges on the question of how one rises to the occasion. The quest narrative reminds us that obstacles may be overcome. It exhibits an "ethic of inspiration . . . rooted in woundedness" but that refuses to give into despair. It entails a belief that something can be gained through the experience of "traveling the distance" to realize an imagined possibility, that a person can turn fate and contingency into "confidence in what is waiting to emerge."[56]

Our use of this narrative archetype raises the question of narrative "truth." Are there not other storylines that we could have employed to tell Melvin's life? In the "chaos" narrative, for example, the protagonist's dilemma is never resolved; there is no happy ending. The plot "doesn't progress by meaningful steps, but winds upon itself, digresses, retreats" and ultimately collapses.[57] The reader will see, however, that while chaos presented itself as a possibility, Melvin held it at bay, although his ability to do so was not simply a matter of individual effort. There were significant others along the way, and enabling institutional resources at his disposal, that gave him the opportunity to imagine and realize a new way of living in the world. Melvin should not be viewed as a supercrip, because his actions were enabled by the social circumstances around him.

Goetting argues that biography is "not simply a 'true' representation of an objective 'reality'" but an incomplete reconstruction of a remembered past that is inevitably marked by a degree of distortion due to the fallibility of memory and the subjectivity of perception.[58] Just as "two people telling a story about the same event may tell it differently," any one person may tell his or her story differently at different points in his or her life.[59] If a story of one's life is told honestly, it may be the closest approximation to the truth that he or she can muster, but it is not the invariant "truth" of what transpired. At the same time, when one tells his or her story from the perspective of hindsight rather than the immediacy of the events, it is no less authentic for having been seasoned by conscious reflection, as *how one remembers* the past may be the most essential part of *the story* that he or she has to tell.[60]

I do not believe that those who tell their life stories should be expected to disclose every intimate detail of their lives. Storytellers, Melvin included, are entitled to some privacy. Indeed, Denzin reminds us that our primary obligation in life-story research is always to the people whose lives we study, "not to our project . . . or discipline. [Their] lives and stories . . . are given to us under a promise . . . that we protect those who have shared with us."[61] Ethical considerations require that we allow the people who tell us their stories to be the final arbiters of what gets told and not told. Besides, as Robert Atkinson observes, a "person's story is essentially an expression of his or her self-understanding. . . . What may be of greatest interest . . . is how [they] see themselves and . . . want others to see them."[62]

Melvin may be a wounded warrior, but he is a warrior nonetheless. He resists those who read his life as a tragedy, and his account does not conform to some preordained therapeutic scheme of grieving over loss, such as Elisabeth Kübler-Ross's stages of denial, anger, bargaining, depression, and acceptance.[63] This narrative of disability—a policing "technology of the self," to borrow a term from Michel Foucault[64]—is one that is imposed on Melvin's life *from without* and does not comport with how he experienced his circumstance *from within*. Like John Hockenberry, who was paralyzed in a car accident during his teenage years, disability taught Melvin "that life could be reinvented. In fact, such an outlook was required. . . . Formulae for change and grief efface the possibility that we might each discover our own way through difficulty, and by doing so reclaim our lives."[65]

Part I **Beginnings**

1. **Roots**

I grew up in Chicago, one among three million people in the third largest city in the United States. The poet Carl Sandburg once called it the "City of the Big Shoulders," as Chicagoans like to do things in a big way. Nestled on the southwest shore of Lake Michigan, Chicago is one of the world's leading industrial and transportation centers and is known for its stunning urban architecture and high-rise buildings, plethora of museums, and enthusiastic sports fans. It is also the place that some of the nation's most notorious gangs call home, the place where my involvement in gangs would forever change my life.[1]

Like many urban areas, Chicago has a large African American population, about 35 to 40 percent of the city's residents during the time of my youth. On the South Side of Chicago, the city's largest section, the majority of residents are black. For the first six and a half years of my life, my family lived on the edge of the South Side, near 113th and Stewart. We lived in a brown and yellow, largely wooden, house. The neighborhood was a suburb of sorts, pleasant and middle-class—mostly houses, a nice community.

Then came the fire. It was just before Christmas of 1976, and there was snow on the ground. My father was at work and my mother had taken my older brother Opie to the store to buy a secret Santa gift for one of his classmates. The store was just two blocks away, and they were only going to be gone a short while. They left me at home with my younger brother Maurice. It was the first time my parents had given me the responsibility of looking after him. I felt pretty good because my mother trusted me enough to leave us alone at home.

While I ate a bowl of cereal in the kitchen, Maurice was playing in another room. He spotted a mouse running through the house and chased it into our parents' bedroom where it ran into a heating duct that was behind a dresser. The dresser was under a big window that was covered with drapes that hung down to the floor.

As a child, Maurice was fascinated with fire and loved playing with matches. When the mouse ran into the duct, Maurice got some matches and threw them in one by one to try to smoke it out. All of a sudden, I smelled smoke from the kitchen. I ran to the bedroom to see what was happening and found the curtains in flames! "What have you done?!" I shouted. "We have to put this fire out!"

I grabbed Maurice by the hand and led him into the kitchen to get water to throw on the fire. We filled several pots full and ran back and forth into the bedroom dousing water on the blaze. It didn't do any good. For some reason, I thought that the cold snow would work better. We ran outside, each grabbed a handful of snow, and rushed back into the house. We threw the snow on the fire, but by now the entire bedroom was engulfed in flames. Maurice stood there mesmerized, a devilish grin on his face. I grabbed him and ran over to our neighbor's house, two doors down the street. Our neighbor called the fire department and the police.

When my mother and Opie returned, fire trucks and police cars had closed off the street a block away. At first, they didn't know which house was on fire. My mother was the first to jump out of the car and run up the street. An officer stopped her and told her there'd been a fire at the brown and yellow house. "Sir, my two boys are in there!" she cried. The officer assured her that we were all right, but that the house had burned to the ground. I felt so terrible because my mother had given me the responsibility of watching Maurice and I had let her—our whole family—down. Our house and all our belongings in it were gone.

As a result of the fire, we moved deeper into South-Side territory, the significance of which I was too young at the time to fathom. For two years, we lived on 63rd and Ingleside, until my parents purchased a duplex on 73rd and Racine. Back then, those were still pretty good neighborhoods, but the move brought me closer to the poorer parts of the city, the rougher kids, and the gangs. My experience with these gangs eventually became the defining feature of my youth, the reason I use a wheelchair today. But I am getting ahead of my story. There is still more to tell of the time before that momentous day when a bullet lodged in my spine, paralyzing me for life.

I spent a lot of my childhood in a place that was entirely different from Chicago—in Shaw, Mississippi, where my parents were born and raised. Shaw is a small, rural town of fewer than 2,000 people in the heart of the Mississippi Delta. The Delta region is known for its fertile lowlands, which have been enriched with silt deposited by river floodwaters, making the soil ideal for the area's large cotton and soybean crops. The work of the soil nourished the "down-home" or country blues in which southern blacks sang about loneliness and sorrow, about struggle and defiance in the face of life's troubles. The blues was the music of a people who suffered, but who worked hard, loved, and persevered.[2] This was the culture of my father's and mother's youth, before they uprooted and migrated north. My parents were from rather large families; my father had four siblings and my mother had seven. They were poor, but they did not lack what they needed. They grew much of their own food and spent most of their days in the fields. If they needed extra money, they chopped cotton for other farmers in the area.

My parents—Cleo Juette, born in 1942, and Shirley Gunn, born in 1943—knew each other from childhood, and they always shared their stories with my brothers and me. My father was an outstanding student and athlete, while my mother was something of a social butterfly. During their high-school years, my father starred on the basketball team, while my mother was a cheerleader. After the games, my father went home to study and even did homework for other students, including my mother, whom he had a crush on since childhood, a sentiment that she did not return in kind. My mother, in turn, went out dancing and hung out with her friends.

After graduating from high school, my mother enrolled in the Mississippi Valley State College, while my father moved to Chicago, following his sister Ernistine, who was the first in our family to move there. In Chicago, my father worked as a taxi driver and later as an insurance salesman. For a while, he did both, until he eventually got a job with the Ford Motor Company, first on the assembly line and later as a quality-control inspector.

During her freshman year in college, my mother got pregnant and had to drop out of school. In 1967, she gave birth to my older brother Torries. Torries was named after my mother's oldest brother, who was hit by a truck and killed while walking along Highway 61, which had no sidewalks. My brother was light skinned with red hair and green eyes, just like the older Torries. He looked like Opie Taylor from the Andy Griffith television show, hence, the nickname Opie, and sometimes people called him Dirty Red.

After Opie's birth, my mother was ready to settle down with a stable man who could provide her with more security. During a return visit to Shaw, my father invited my mother and her newborn son to come live with him in Chicago. Shortly after that, they were married. I was born on May 18, 1969, and Maurice was born a year and a half later. Soon my parents bought their first home, the one on 113th and Stewart that Maurice later burned down.

For as long as I can remember, everyone called me Boonie. My mother gave me this nickname—one of her best friends had a daughter named Boonie. No one in the family seems to know anything about the origins of the name or what it's supposed to mean, but people back in Shaw often teased me for being named after a girl.

I spent a good part of my early childhood exposed to my family's Mississippi roots. At the time, my parents were still struggling financially, and my father's mother, Luelle, took care of me for the better part of my first two years of life. I even received some of my early schooling in Shaw, completing the second grade under the tutelage of one of my parents' teachers, Miss Bell. My brothers and I also spent several summers in Shaw, much of the time without our parents, who dropped us off and returned to Chicago, leaving us with other grandmothers.

My grandmother, Luelle, was a short woman of African American and Native American descent with striking facial features. She was very fond of me, and I felt like I was her favorite grandson. Some of my best childhood memories are of us working in her garden and of rounding up the baby chicks and picking them up or chasing them into their roost. We gave the chicks names and kept track of how many we caught. I also played in the fields and pasture and ran around town with the other local boys who liked to pick fruit off the many trees that adorned Luelle's yard. My grandmother wasn't too keen on this practice, for the kids were impatient and often ate unripe fruit that made them sick—a rather minor delinquency compared to the stuff we later got into in Chicago.

One of the things I remember most about Shaw is the popularity of my mother's side of the family. My grandmother, Nancy, whom we called Mama, had accumulated enough savings with my now deceased grandfather to invest in a half dozen houses, which my grandmother continued to rent. My mother's older brother, Tommy, was a talented carpenter who had helped build the local high school. When anyone heard the Gunn name, they always said, "Tommy Gunn's the one who built the high school." In those days, it was a big deal for a black man to have built a high school, and Tommy was highly revered. The Gunn family also had a reputation for helping others in need. It seemed that everyone knew the Gunns. People routinely approached me and said, "You're Shirley Gunn's son, ain't you?"

As a middle child, I was always much closer to Opie, whom I looked up to, than to Maurice. During our Mississippi visits, Opie and I stayed with one of our grandmothers while Maurice stayed with my mother's older sister, Maureen. Aunt Maureen loved Maurice and spoiled him rotten, dressing him in cute little suits. She lived in another town, so we didn't see much of Maurice during our summer visits. But when Maurice did come to visit, Aunt Maureen wouldn't let him play with Opie and me because we wore ragged clothes and liked to wrestle and roll around in the dirt. Because of Aunt Maureen, Maurice thought he was better than Opie and me, which of course annoyed us to no end.

For many years, I enjoyed my visits to Shaw—until the summer of 1982. I was thirteen years old and had just completed the seventh grade. By then, the slower pace of rural life began to bore me, and I wanted to spend my time hanging out with my friends and my girlfriend. Over our protests, however, my parents took my brothers and me down to Shaw for the summer. It would be the last time they did this. They expected us to work for my mother's younger brother, Lonnie, in his restaurant. Uncle Lonnie told us we could have all the food we could eat, but we wouldn't be paid. My mother had told everyone in the family not to give us any money because she knew we only wanted to earn enough to catch a bus back to Chicago.

Opie and I felt trapped. Opie figured we needed about seventy dollars to pay for the bus trip and some food along the way. We started thinking about ways to make money. Our first idea was to collect pop bottles and cans. We collected about twenty dollars but spent all of it on candy and other incidentals. Then a friend told us about how we could earn a lot of money by chopping cotton in the fields. It sounded easy enough, but Grandma Nancy, Mama, tried to talk us out of it: "Y'all don't know what y'all gettin' into. If y'all serious about this, I better go along."

Mama woke Opie and me around 4:30 a.m. and made us breakfast before we went out to meet the truck that came through Shaw at 5:00 a.m. to pick up the workers and take everyone to the fields. I remember the other workers saying, "Hi, Mrs. Gunn, are these your grandkids? Is this their first time going to the fields?" They could tell right away that Opie and I were city boys. We were dressed in shorts, tank tops, and baseball caps, while they all wore several layers of clothes to keep the bugs away and large sombreros to protect them from the sun.

The work was a lot harder than we thought it would be. We picked cotton for four hours before we had our first break. Then the water truck came out and returned every two hours until the workday was over in the late afternoon. Opie and I were completely exhausted; our backs hurt from bending over and our hands were raw from holding the hoe. "How the hell did the slaves do this?" I thought. "If I were a slave, they'd have to shoot me before I did this shit everyday."

Needless to say, we didn't earn enough money to get back to Chicago. But this was the last time I went down to Mississippi for many years. I vowed never to return without my own car, so I could leave any time I wanted.

My father is a quiet and stoic man who always worked hard to provide for our family and set a good example for my brothers and me. We were lucky because most of the kids in my neighborhood had fathers who weren't involved in their lives. Still, there is little doubt that my mother has been the driving force in our family. She is a strong black woman, passionate and loving but boisterous and opinionated. When she walks into a room, she commands respect. She is also a devout Baptist and made sure we were steeped in the church.

Every Sunday morning we had to get up by 7:00 a.m. to get ready for a full day at the Evening Star Missionary Baptist Church that began at 9:00 a.m. I remember my brothers and I scurrying around the house looking for our socks and shoes as we tried to get ready. First, we went to Sunday school—my mother was one of the teachers —followed by a school breakfast. Then we attended services with the entire congregation from 11:00 a.m. to 3:00 p.m. After that, we usually had a reception to celebrate some occasion and then an afternoon program that lasted until 7:00 p.m.

Although it could be a long day, I enjoyed my time and appreciated the nurturing structure of the church. Even after I became involved in gangs, I still served as an usher and a junior deacon and brought my friends to Sunday services. My religious upbringing didn't prevent me from getting into trouble—I knew right from wrong but didn't always obey—but along with my family ties, it did keep me grounded and prevent me from doing something too criminally severe.

Perhaps my fondest memories of church are the times I spent gospel singing in the church choir. Often we visited other churches to sing and compete with other choirs for recognition as the best singing group. The rivalries between choirs could get pretty intense as we kept trying to outdo each other. Often we'd sing additional songs not scheduled on the program in order to impress the congregation with our virtuoso ability.

My mother actually harbored hopes that the "Juette Family" could become another Jackson Five. But she made the mistake of putting all her hope in Maurice, thinking that since Michael, the youngest of the Jacksons, was the star of the Jackson Five, her youngest son should be the star of our group. Although Maurice could sing well, he often suffered from stage fright. Every time we visited a church to perform, we went through the same routine with Maurice.

"Maurice, are you gonna sing today?" my mother gently coaxed.

"I don't wanna sing," Maurice whined.

"I'll buy you that car you want."

"I don't wanna car. I'm not gonna sing."

Then my mother, who was prone to emotional, verbal outbursts, would lose her patience: "If you don't sing, Maurice, I'm gonna whup your goddamn ass."

When we lived on 113th and Stewart, Maurice and I shared a bedroom in the attic that my parents had remodeled. I remember being scared of the adjacent room in the attic that we used for storage. It was dark and creepy, and we never went in there. There was a life-size painting of Bozo the Clown on the door, and when the outside street lights shined on the door at night, it made Bozo's face light up like a ghost, which terrified me.

For the most part, my brothers and I got along fairly well. Opie was the unquestioned leader, as we adhered to a family pecking order based on seniority, and Maurice and I generally went along with whatever Opie told us to do. Occasionally, however, Maurice would get a little uppity—such as when he had a birthday and became a year older —and I had to give him a little beating to put him in his place.

One time, when Maurice and I were playing in our upstairs room, he slipped by the door and tumbled down the spiral staircase, bouncing off the wall. I thought that it was the funniest thing I had ever seen. Maurice received a couple of bruises but wasn't hurt, and we both laughed about it so hard that I had tears in my eyes. When Opie came home, I told him that Maurice had done a somersault down the stairs, and Opie insisted that he do it again! This time around it wasn't so funny, and Maurice got banged up pretty badly.

Perhaps because he was sometimes the "odd man out," Maurice developed a family reputation as a troublemaker, the "bad one" among the three brothers. This reputation was in no small part due to his interest in matches. But Maurice was also the mischievous type— he'd break things, mess up his room, throw clothes all over the place, and refuse to clean it up. As for me, I was generally a quiet youth, much like my father, and tried to stay below my parents' radar.

Opie and I took advantage of Maurice's reputation, and we conspired to blame him for any trouble we got into. In those early years, the trouble wasn't too serious—one of us would raid the cookie jar when we weren't supposed to, break a plate or drinking glass, or lose a piece of sporting equipment. But when something like this happened, our parents assembled us in a lineup and interrogated us about "who did it." Opie was the first to respond, "I didn't do it." Then I chimed in, "I didn't do it." But when Maurice said, "I didn't do it," he got blamed nonetheless.

Our parents, like their parents before them, used well-intentioned physical punishment to discipline us. Our father's preferred method was a whupping with a belt. I don't know what was worse, the actual whupping or the emotional stress of anticipation as we made the long trip down the hallway to receive our punishment. At first, my brothers and I tried to avoid crying, taking pride and boasting to each other about our bravery. Eventually we realized that we were better off if we pretended to cry because this would end the ordeal more quickly. Thus, I started breaking out in tears immediately, a couple of times even before the belt hit me.

At the same time, we actually feared our mother's verbal tirades more than a whupping with the belt. Her yelling and screaming was intimidating and had the added effect of making us feel guilty about whatever we'd done. The three of us learned to keep a safe distance from her, for she also might smack us if we got too close when she was in this state of mind. To this day, we live in fear of being on the receiving end of one of her verbal assaults. Unlike our father, who'd react to a transgression immediately, our mother often let things simmer before confronting us about some wrongdoing. I was bewildered when she'd bring it up later, long after we thought we'd gotten away with it. Then, one day, something would get her upset. She'd start off

The Juette family (2005). *Left to right:* Melvin, Opie, Shirley, Cleo, and Maurice.

in the bedroom, cursing at my father. Then she'd go to Opie's room and curse him out. Then to Maurice's and my room.

My brothers and I learned how to manipulate our mother, too. If she grounded us for some misbehavior, we'd play basketball in our room, using a sock as a ball and a clothes hanger as a basket. When we'd get too loud, she'd come in and say we couldn't play basketball anymore. Then we'd move our beds around and play football, jumping back and forth from bed to bed and throwing our clothes all over the place. Our mother would get so frustrated that she'd kick us out of the house and tell us not to come back until suppertime.

In many ways, however, our mother was more tolerant of our troublemaking than our father, who was always more judgmental. She even protected us from him at times. I remember the time my parents let me drive their new Chevrolet for the entire day. It was a privilege they granted in celebration of my sixteenth birthday. I had just gotten my learner's permit and was excited about getting behind the wheel.

Accompanied by Opie and an older friend, Dobby Daniels, I drove east on 75th Street toward Chicago Vocational High School for my driver education class. I was driving with both hands on the wheel, like I had been taught, when Dobby teased me, "Boonie, chill out, you look like a nerd. You don't need to drive with two hands. Lean to the side a little bit. Turn up the music."

I thought I was pretty cool rolling along with my gangster lean as we kicked it, talked, and listened to the music. But I was driving too fast and pumping the brakes to avoid hitting the woman driving the car in front of me. Dobby told me to stop tailgating, but I didn't know what he meant. Suddenly at the next stoplight, I slammed into the woman's car, which, in turn, hit the next car in front. I was in shock, in a daze, and just sat there with both hands on the wheel. I couldn't believe I was involved in an accident in my parents' new car! Dobby and Opie got out of the car first to talk to the woman I'd hit. I finally got up the nerve to get out, too. I saw that the woman's car had received only minor damage and that the lead car was unscathed. But the front grill of our new Chevy was completely smashed.

I was too nervous to drive back home, so Dobby drove the car. All I could think about was that my father would kill me and that I should run away. When we got home, Dobby pulled the car over to the curb. My mother came out of the house. She already knew what happened because the woman had called her and told her about the accident.

"Are y'all okay?" my mother asked. When she saw that everyone was fine, she told me, "Boonie, you better pray to God that the brakes gave out and you couldn't stop."

"No, I was tailgating," I replied, trying to be honest.

"You hear me," she insisted. "You better pray to God that the goddamn brakes gave out and you couldn't stop."

When my father got home from work, my mother met him in front of the house and told him that the brakes had gone out. "I thought they felt funny when I drove the other day," she said. My father never disagreed with her; he just stayed calm and absorbed whatever she had to say. I'm certain he knew that the accident had nothing to do with the brakes, but he never said anything more about it. He just asked me if I was all right. Then he threw me the car keys and told me to pull the Chevy into the driveway. All I could think was, "Thank God he's still going to let me drive."

2. **In the Company of Peers**

After the fire that destroyed our home in 1976, we moved into a one-bedroom apartment near 63rd and Ingleside, where we lived for a year and a half, until my parents saved enough money to buy a duplex near 73rd and Racine. At that time, the younger kids on the South Side of Chicago were not yet involved in gangs, and the older ones who were in gangs were not yet packing guns. Still, the kids in this part of the city were rougher than the ones I had known on 113th and Stewart, and I soon learned that I had to fight in order to get by.

The first fight I remember getting into was at a playground near our apartment. I had climbed up to the top of a swing to unravel the chain that some of the older kids had wrapped around the horizontal bar to keep the younger kids from using it. When I got down, a kid my age named Richard jumped onto the swing before I had a chance to get on it. I confronted him: "Man, what are you doing? Get the hell out of my swing." Richard looked at me but didn't say anything. Standing nearby was his friend, Derrick, who egged Richard on:

"Man, fuck him. That's your swing." But I walked over to Richard, hit him squarely in the face, and knocked him out of the swing, kicking him several more times while he was on the ground. Then he jumped up, and the two of them ran off.

I was lucky that being a good fighter came naturally to me. I was also an athletic youth, lean and muscular. Perhaps hanging out with my older brother had toughened me up, too. I was confident that I could take care of myself on the street.

About a week after the swing incident, Derrick and Richard reappeared at the park. Derrick approached me first and started up a friendly conversation. Richard soon followed suit. The three of us became good friends, forming our own little gang and fighting against kids from the adjacent neighborhood. We were inseparable during the time that I lived in that area of town.

Things did not always come easy for me, however. After moving to 73rd and Racine, I enrolled in Amos Alonzo Stagg elementary school. On my first day at school, I threw up. I don't know if I was sick or nervous, but there was something about the smell of the place that made me nauseated; it smelled like urine and disinfectant. There couldn't have been a worse way to be introduced to a new group of classmates. Everyone called me the Little Throw-up Boy, and besides the teasing, they'd have nothing to do with me.

I gravitated to another boy named Lavelle, a short kid who was also an outcast. The other students always picked on Lavelle. During recess, Lavelle and I stayed inside and worked on jigsaw puzzles together. We had spent several weeks working on this one puzzle, and when it was almost completed, Steve, the class bully, came over to us and took the puzzle completely apart.

"What'cha do that for?" Lavelle protested.

"What'cha gonna do about it?" Steve taunted, as he pushed Lavelle.

"Knock it off!" I said, as I got up from my chair.

"What'cha gonna do about it, Throw-up Boy?" Steve retorted.

I wanted to punch Steve in his face. But I did nothing; I backed down. It wasn't that I was afraid of Steve. I'd promised my mother that I'd be on my best behavior at the new school, and I didn't want to get a whupping at home if I got into a fight. But Steve thought I was scared, and everyday for the next two weeks he tried to pick a fight.

Then one day he followed me into the bathroom at recess, accompanied by another kid named Gregory, and locked the door behind them. Gregory, who had broken his leg and was using crutches, was apparently there to witness the beating Steve planned to give me. Steve approached me and said, "So, Throw-up Boy, you think you're tough shit?"

"I ain't messin' with you," I replied. "Get out of my face."

Then Steve pushed me back against the wall. I could've tolerated his teasing and taunting, but I couldn't let him push me like that. I swung at him, hitting him in the face several times and knocking him to the ground. Steve started crying and then got up and ran back to the classroom. "You really beat the crap out of Steve," said Gregory, amazed and impressed. I just gave him a stern look and walked out the door as he followed me back to the room.

When we returned, we saw Steve sitting at his desk with his face down trying to hide his tears. Everyone came up to Gregory and me to find out what happened. "Throw-up Boy beat the mess out of Steve!" explained Gregory, as he told them in vivid detail what had happened. I won the respect of everyone in the class. They didn't particularly like Steve either, but they were afraid of him. After that incident, they stopped teasing Lavelle and me. They were friendlier and started playing with us and helping us put together the puzzle.

Like most boys, I loved to play sports—baseball, football, and basketball. This is what my brothers, friends, and I did everyday. We played in organized church groups, in Little League and Pony League, and in neighborhood pick-up games. I often fantasized about what it would be like to hit a grand slam in the bottom of the ninth to win the World Series, catch a touchdown pass to win the Super Bowl, or make a shot at the buzzer to win an NBA championship

We played games against kids from other neighborhoods, the same ones who would become our gang rivals when we got older. We competed for bragging rights over whose neighborhood was the best. The games inevitably led to arguments and fistfights. For me, fighting was part of the fun. I knew that I could count on my brothers and my friends, and they could count on me, for backup in a fight. There was something exciting about the battle, about fighting the good fight, and something admirable about the camaraderie and loyalty that we all felt toward each other.

I have always been a pretty talented athlete. Later, during high school, I played on the football team for a while. I was very fast; I could run the forty-yard dash in 4.2 seconds, but I didn't have the discipline to stay with it. Three times I quit the team only to return. The coach put up with me because I was such a good player and an asset to the team when I was on the field.

Earlier, while playing baseball in the large backyard of our duplex, I met the boy who would become my best friend. It was a beautiful summer day. Maurice was pitching, and Opie hit a fly into the alley that bordered the back of our lot. Kim Evans, a tall, lanky kid, happened to be walking by, chest out, strutting like a peacock, when the ball hit him squarely on the side of his head.[1]

When we first moved to the neighborhood, the residents had warned us about Kim, who was a year younger than me. Kim, they said, was a troublemaker, a badass, always getting into fights with other kids.

As I ran into the alley to retrieve the ball, I found Kim holding it in his hands. "Who hit me with this motherfuckin' ball?!" he exclaimed angrily.

"I'm sorry, we're just playing baseball," I replied. "Just give me the ball."

"Naw, I ain't gonna give you shit," Kim said, jutting out his chest.

By now I'd gotten to the point of never backing down from a fight if I was provoked, and I punched Kim in the face and took the ball. He was stunned. With tears in his eyes, he retreated, if only temporarily.

Kim came from a large family; he had thirteen brothers and sisters. In a few minutes, he returned with some of his sisters. One of his sisters said, "Kim, is this him? You wanna finish kicking his ass now?" Kim hesitated and then said, "No, I think he had enough."

By standing up to Kim, I had won his respect, and from then on, he came over to the house almost every day. My brothers and I were glad to have an extra person to make even teams for our ballgames. Over time, Kim became my best friend, practically a member of the family. Even when my mother grounded me for something I'd done wrong, she'd still let Kim come over. And if Kim cursed or otherwise misbehaved in our home, she'd put him on punishment, too. She'd call Kim's mother, who'd tell her, "Fine, don't send him home until he finishes his punishment," which might've entailed cleaning up our garage or basement. Kim's mother, in turn, would treat us the same way if we did something wrong in her home.

In those days, the neighbors looked after each other's children. If one of the adults saw a kid doing something wrong, they told their parents. And we kids, even after we got involved in gangs, were still respectful of our elders. Things are totally different today, as the entire fabric of the community has changed. Most of the original homeowners who previously formed a network of supportive neighbors have passed away. Where there were once homes, there are now many vacant lots. The adults in the area are more hesitant to get involved in another family's business, and the kids have little respect for their elders.

Around the seventh grade, I became interested in girls. My friends and I threw parties in our basement and planned in advance which girl each of us wanted to hook up with. We served chips, listened to music, and just hung and talked. If the girls were willing, we played "Catch a Girl, Kiss a Girl"—a hide-'n'-seek game played with the lights out, where each boy tried to find the particular girl he liked. My mother kept tabs on us by listening through a trap door that was in the bathroom above the basement. If it got too quiet, she banged on the door and shouted, "What's going on down there?" If it got too noisy, she banged on it, too.

My parents never talked to me about sex, and most of what I learned came from Opie and the older guys in the neighborhood, who bragged about how many girls they had slept with and how much the girls loved them. Having a reputation as a player with the girls was even more important than having a reputation as a good fighter. My friends and I looked up to these guys and wanted to follow in their footsteps.

I did receive some sex education in school, but I didn't find it particularly helpful. The teacher showed us diagrams of fallopian tubes and such, but we'd just say, "We already know *how* to have sex. What's this got to do with it?" Most of us were less knowledgeable about sex than we made out to be, however. Although we may have boasted about having intercourse, most of us exaggerated, and those of us who did never thought about using birth control. As for me, sex at that age was mainly petting. I might get naked with a girl and press my body against hers—because that's what I thought I was supposed to do—but it was some time before I had intercourse or even an orgasm. Still, it was sex, and sex was the cool thing to do. If your friends thought you were a virgin, or at least not sexually active in some way, they continually teased you.

My first serious girlfriend was Kathy. I often brought Kathy over to the house and took her down to the basement to "make out." When we were ready to leave, Kim was waiting outside to tease me. "Was it fun, Boonie? Was it fun? Did you get her? Did you fuck her?" he chanted. And to the tune of "Take Me Out to the Ballgame," he sang, "Three strikes and you're out at the old sex game."

Often my friends and I went to the mall to try to score as many phone numbers as possible. We'd come back home, line up the numbers, and call up the girls. We made a contest out of who could get the prettiest girls and how many of them we could get to go out, and have sex, with us.

Dances and parties were also occasions to meet girls, especially when we were older. On Saturday afternoons, we went to dances at the Skyway, a lounge for thirteen- to seventeen-year-olds. On Friday and Saturday nights, we went to dances at the local high school or parties at private residences, the latter primarily when someone's parents weren't at home. The host at these parties invested in a disc jockey and sold tickets for a dollar at the door. Opie and I hosted these parties as often as we could.

Besides an ability to sweet-talk the girls, it was also important to demonstrate verbal prowess with male peers by threatening to "whup your ass" or by teasing or insulting someone about their physical appearance, sexual inexperience, sexual orientation, or relatives. Insulting a person's mother was the most provocative thing one could do. Other relatives were fair game, but not mothers. Many a fight broke out after such a disparaging remark. It took considerable verbal skill to respond in kind without resorting to physical violence. We measured each other's mental agility and toughness by the humor and creativity of our verbal repartee.[2]

Break-dancing was another one of our competitive pursuits. This acrobatic dance style, which has become a staple of hip-hop culture, broke onto the Chicago scene in the early 1980s. We often had competitions, or battles, in which we tried to show each other up by performing more creative and complex maneuvers on successive, alternative turns. Audiences gathered around—on the street and in arcades and nightclubs—to cheer us on. The dancers who received the loudest cheers were declared the winner.

Modesty aside, I was a really good break-dancer, the best in my neighborhood. Dressed in my red and black Puma jogging suit, I took on all comers. Guys from other neighborhoods came to challenge me. At first, I simply trash-talked them, saying I wouldn't waste my time doing battle with them. They had to beat my little brother first before they earned the right to take me on.

My battle strategy was to save my best move for last. I laid back, waiting to see what my opponent could do. The dances typically began with some fancy footwork, followed by more complex moves such as a head spin or windmill. In the latter, the dancer spins from his upper back to his chest while twirling his legs rapidly around his body in a V shape. While most of my opponents could only perform this move with their hands pushing off the ground, I could do it with my hands raised behind my back and legs. As the winner of the battle, I was entitled to the other guy's Puma jacket or shoes.

In many respects, I was less impulsive than many of my friends. I thought things through more, about the consequences of our actions, and tried to keep the other guys from doing something too deviant or outlandish. I think this had a lot to do with my parents and religious upbringing. Fighting with other youths who got what they deserved was one thing, but unprovoked violence or thievery was another matter. Besides, I didn't need to steal to get what I wanted. My parents were good financial providers, and I earned extra money by cutting the neighbors' grass or shoveling snow during the winter. For a time, my mother worked as manager in the boys' section of a major department store. Every Friday after school, my brothers and I helped her sort and stock the newly arrived clothes. While she didn't pay us, she did pull out the best clothes in the shipment and bought them for us at wholesale prices.

My older cousin, Larry Gunn, on the other hand, was the instigator of our group. He was always trying to talk the younger guys into doing things that I disapproved of. My mother always warned me about Larry. She called him a "snake," an "evil spirit," someone who was "just plain low-down."

Kim was especially susceptible to Larry's provocations. There was the time when Larry tried to talk Kim into running a train, a gang rape, on one of Kim's girlfriends. "Man, she ain't nothin' but a bitch," Larry taunted. "You scared, motherfucker? Ain't you a player? Let's do this. All you have to do is turn off the lights, get up when you're done, and tell her you're going to the bathroom. Then I'll get on top of her and she won't even know it's me."

Kim was intimidated and seemed like he was going to give in to Larry. But I told him, "Man, fuck Larry, don't listen to him. If you do it, that's rape. Your dumb ass will end up in jail." To be honest, at the time, I didn't even know this girl very well and didn't really care about her. But I didn't want Kim to get arrested, and since they were planning to use my house, I didn't want to get into trouble either. Fortunately, Kim, who did like this girl, listened to me.

My friends also went through a phase when Larry convinced them that stealing bikes from younger kids who lived in other neighborhoods was a cool thing to do. They'd take a bus over to the forest preserve and wait for a kid to ride down the trail. Then they would jump the kid and steal his bike. They each kept a bike for themselves and sold the rest, and what they couldn't sell, they used for spare parts.

It seemed that everyone in my neighborhood except Kim and I had one of these stolen bikes. So we decided to take the bus over to the forest preserve and get ourselves one, too. We spent most of the day waiting for someone to ride down the trail, but no one came. Since we were out of money for the bus, we started walking back home. As we were walking, we spotted a younger boy riding toward us on the sidewalk. Just as he was about to pass, I reached over and knocked the handlebars of his bike, causing him to flip over. I looked down at this helpless kid and for a moment seriously thought about taking his bike. But I felt sorry for him and instead simply asked, "Are you okay?" I helped him back onto his bike and sent him on his way. Kim complained all the way home: "Man, we should have took the bike." But my heart wasn't into doing something like this.

Some of the older neighborhood boys also liked to steal merchandise from the cargo trains that regularly passed through the area. The cargo included everything from small refrigerators to microwaves, TV sets, and Nike gym shoes. The trains were long and slow moving, and no security guards were on board. At a spot on 74th Street between Racine and Morgan, in a wooded area of town, you could actually jump onto the cars, break the lock, and get inside. The guys on the train then handed, or gently threw, the merchandise down to accomplices on the ground. If the stuff was too big to catch, they just let it drop. There were a lot of bushes in the area, which cushioned the shock as the boxes hit the turf. To be sure, a lot of things broke, but much of it survived intact. I occasionally bought merchandise that had been taken from the trains, but I never stole anything myself.

Sometimes the police spotted the boys hanging around the tracks as the trains passed by. In those instances, the boys stashed the loot in the woods and ran off, and the cops thought they were just kids who wanted to ride the trains. Later they returned to pick up what they had left behind.

Along with my disinterest in thievery, I never seriously got into alcohol or drugs. I liked to keep mentally alert and physically ready in case I needed to fight. There are only two incidents that I recall in which I got stone-cold drunk.

The first one occurred when I was about eight years old. There was a bar in the basement family room where we played, but the bar was, of course, off limits to my brothers and me. On that day, my mother was out of town and my father wasn't keeping very close tabs on us. We decided to go over to the bar and started drinking the alcohol. That's when things got out of control. We hooted and hollered, sang and danced, and made a mess of the basement, throwing toys all over the place. We tried doing some laundry in the adjacent laundry room, which was normally off-limits to us, and clogged up the washing machine so badly that water overflowed and spilled onto the floor. Then we took the wet laundry out of the machine and threw it all over the floor.

Our father heard the commotion and came down to investigate. When he saw what we had done, he was seething with anger. "Clean up this shit!" he demanded. "And when you're done, y'all come upstairs and I'm gonna whup your asses!"

The three of us stood there stunned as our father went back upstairs. Then we started the tedious task of cleaning up the mess. Maurice, however, went back over to the bar and began drinking again. When our father came back down to check on us, Opie and I were working diligently while Maurice was on top of the bar laughing and singing. Our father looked scornfully at Maurice: "Oh, you don't think fat meat is greasy? You come and get your ass whupping now." He grabbed Maurice and took him upstairs. A few moments later, we heard Maurice crying out in pain. We knew he wasn't faking.

Neither Opie nor I were looking forward to going upstairs. We kept on cleaning and recleaning the basement, hoping that if everything looked perfect maybe our father would go easy on us. We stayed down there several more hours, and by the time we went upstairs our father was asleep. We crept quietly into our bedrooms and went to sleep, too. The next morning our father came into the kitchen for breakfast, looked at us with a sly smile, and said, "Y'all got away from me last night, didn't you? I owe y'all one."

My second experience with binge drinking occurred many years later, when I was about fifteen years old, in the aftermath of a fire that had scorched a neighborhood liquor store. After an insurance agent took an inventory of the damaged merchandise, the owner of the store told one of my friends, Hucoro, that we could take all the soot-stained beer cans and liquor bottles we wanted. One morning after my father left for work, Hucoro and I went over to the liquor store and filled several garbage bags with alcohol. We brought the bags back to my house and started washing off the soot. We invited some of our other friends to join us, and we drank all day long. Later in the day, Kim and I went over to a girlfriend's house. I remember sitting on the porch talking shit to a bunch of guys who were laughing at me because I was so drunk. I fell down the porch stairs, picked myself up, and headed toward home. The last thing I remember was walking down the street, a pint of liquor in every pocket, sloppy drunk, falling down all over the place, feeling sick, and throwing up.

Someone found me passed out in the alley and went over to the house to tell Opie where I was. Opie dragged me back home and rolled me into bed. My head was pounding furiously as I vomited all over myself and my bed. Opie cleaned up the mess with a towel and got me a garbage bag to keep by my bed. When our father came back from work and saw the state I was in, all he said was, "You had to learn the hard way, huh."

I slept for nearly two days, and when I finally awoke, I had the worst hangover you could imagine. I went into the kitchen and found one of my friends drinking and washing the soot off of some beer cans and liquor bottles. When I smelled the alcohol, I threw up again. After that experience, I never wanted to feel that way again.

3. Gangs

There was no distinct moment when I suddenly thought, "Okay, as of today, I'm in a gang." It happened gradually, as I got into fights and learned who my friends and enemies were.[1] But Opie and Dobby Daniels were clearly the ones who drew me further into this world.

It all seems to have started when I was in the eighth grade, my last year at Alonzo Stagg. Opie and Dobby were already attending Chicago Vocational High School, or CVS as we called it. Dobby was a charismatic youth and one of the biggest guys in the neighborhood, 6'3" and muscular, the star quarterback of the CVS football team. If he ever needed backup for a fight, he could count on his teammates for help.

Dobby worked as a disc jockey at parties. He'd bought the DJ equipment that he needed with the help of his mother, who had a good job at the post office and was known to spoil her son. Dobby's mother also helped him buy a big yellow and chrome Fleetwood Cadillac, which he fixed up in the CVS auto shop. The flashy vehicle was a status symbol. When Opie and I rode around with Dobby, we could be assured of being noticed, and we felt cool and respected. At first, I didn't pay much attention to the gang signs that Dobby threw out the window when we drove past a group of Gangster Disciples (GDs); I wasn't quite aware of what I was getting myself into. At the time, the GDs was the principal gang in our neighborhood. But at CVS, Dobby chose to hang out with members of the Black P Stones (BPSs), a rival gang from another area. (The P stands for peace.) Because of this affiliation with the BPSs, Dobby often fought with the GDs.

Dobby liked having his own neighborhood gang, which meant he didn't have to rely on his high-school friends to back him up in a fight. For Opie and me, this was a dangerous alliance.

Dobby treated me like family and introduced me to his BPS friends as his little brother or cousin. "Boonie's straight. He's from my neighborhood," Dobby would say. So it was natural for the GDs to assume I had joined up with the BPSs, and they continually challenged me either to switch my allegiance or fight. They allowed no neutral ground; you were either with them or against them. A lot of the kids decided to join gangs mainly because they were threatened with beatings if they refused. My friends and I banded together to protect ourselves against the GDs.

I remember getting taunted by some GDs for refusing to join up with them: They'd shout, "King Shorty gonna shoot you in the legs!" King Shorty was a tough neighborhood kid named Anton. I'd played with Anton on a Pony League baseball team, but at the time, I didn't know that Anton and King Shorty were one and the same. I did know, however, that Anton was a GD, and one day we got into a fight. He was acting crazy and yelling, "I'm King Shorty! I'm gonna whup your ass! I'm gonna kill you!"

"You're King Shorty?!" I replied. "You're the punk who's supposed to shoot me! I'm gonna beat *your* ass!"

I was angry and beat up Anton pretty badly. He went back to his gang friends, told them that he'd been jumped by a bunch of BPSs and urged them to retaliate. Fortunately, I was friends with a guy named

Pee Wee. All Pee Wee's brothers were GDs, and one of them, T.C., called the shots for the GDs in the neighborhood. Since we all knew each other, T.C. protected me for a while.

The whole business of gang rivalries and alliances can get rather complicated. Although it may seem rather peculiar to outsiders, gang members take it all very seriously. After the fight, Anton began calling my friends and me the Hooks on Racine. Gang members use derogatory terms to refer to rival gangs and various symbols to represent their group and mark their territory with graffiti. The cane is a symbol of the Vice Lords (VLs), a large Chicago gang that is aligned with the BPSs. If you turn a cane upside down, which is a sign of disrespect, it looks like a hook. Thus, Anton dubbed us the Hooks on Racine.

Pee Wee's brother Neil was the first gang member to teach me about gang symbols and etiquette. I learned that the GDs used a six-pointed star to represent their group. If a GD asked you to "split the star," you had to know that the six points stood for "love, live, loyalty, wisdom, knowledge, and understanding." If you didn't know the answer, you could get beaten. Such were the rules of the streets that I came from.

Street lore and published accounts suggest that the BPSs, the gang that I aligned with, was founded by two youths named Jeff Fort and Eugene Hariston in 1959. The group, which was originally called the Blackstone Rangers, consisted of youths who lived around Blackstone Avenue and 63rd and 65th Streets in the Woodlawn area of the South Side. Over the next decade, some fifty neighborhood gangs with about six thousand members claimed affiliation with the larger group, now called the Black P Stone Nation, with Fort designated as the "Black Prince" of the nation.[2]

During the civil rights era of the 1960s, Fort cultivated an image of the BPSs as a socially conscious, self-help organization that could advance the cause of impoverished African Americans. In 1969, he obtained a $1.4 million federal antipoverty grant that he used to support the group's illegal enterprises, which now included drug trafficking. In 1972, Fort was convicted of defrauding the government and served four and a half years in prison. Following his release, he transformed the group into a Black Muslim cover organization called El Rukn, which operates both legal and illegal enterprises to this very day. In the 1980s, El Rukn became affiliated with a broader coalition of gangs, or sets, that are known as the People Nation.

Gang coalitions like the People Nation typically form in state penitentiaries, when inmates from different neighborhoods are brought together under one roof and form cooperative economic and protection rackets inside the prison. These associations are then used to organize illegal activities on the street. Contemporary People gangs include groups such as the VLs, El Rukn, Latin Kings, Four Corner Hustlers, and Cobra Stones, as well as the BPSs.

The BPSs' rival, the Black Disciples, was apparently started in the mid-1960s by David Barksdale, who joined forces with Larry Hoover to form the Black Gangster Disciple Nation. At the point of merger, Barksdale was designated as "King," with Hoover second in command. In 1972, Barksdale died of complications from gunshot wounds that he received a couple years earlier. Several influential members fought with Hoover for control of the organization, causing splits in the gang. By the 1980s, groups variously known as Black Disciples, Black GDs, GDs, and Latin Disciples, among others, aligned to form the Folks Nation, in opposition to the People Nation. People and Folks are Chicago's—and by now other areas of the Midwest as well—version of the Crips and Bloods, the infamous gangs of Los Angeles area communities.

People and Folks gang members employ an elaborate set of symbols to communicate with each other. People wear gang-identifying ornaments and clothing on their left side—such as an earring, a rolled-up pant leg, a dangling overall strap, and a tilted baseball cap.

Folks wear these identifiers to the right. People use a five-pointed star for their graffiti markings, while Folks use a six-pointed star. There are also a number of other symbols—canes, crowns, hats, pitchforks, pyramids, among others—that the groups use in their graffiti to symbolically assert control over particular neighborhood turfs.

Although these two coalitions comprise the main gang rivalries in Chicago, groups within each alliance also fight with each other. Like nations in international disputes, they are often aligned more by their common enemies than their common bonds.

If there was one incident, a key turning point, that cemented my involvement in gangs, it was on a cold Christmas Eve in 1983. Every year, WBMX, a local radio station, threw a big Christmas party at a downtown hotel. My mother didn't want me to go, but Opie talked her into letting me. Although you were supposed to be seventeen or older to get in, it was easy to pass through the door. People from all over the city would be there, and we thought that it would be a great opportunity to pick up girls. Unfortunately, a lot of gang members would be there, too.

Opie and I took a bus with our friend, George Harper. At the party, we met up with David Mauldin, and David's older brother, Paul. Paul had already graduated from high school and had a job as a security guard at the downtown public library. Although Paul was no longer an active gang member, he had been involved with the VLs. He still wore two diamond earrings on his left ear.

As the party was winding down, a fight broke out between members of the People-affiliated VLs and the Folk-affiliated GDs. Things were getting out of hand, and we decided that we better leave. After we'd walked a few blocks to catch the El (Chicago's above-ground train system) back to the South Side, we realized there were lots of GDs in the area. Paul told us, "If we run into any trouble and have to separate, we can meet at the library. My buddies are working the night shift. They'll let us in. If I say 'break,' take off running."

It wasn't long before we were confronted by a group of GDs. "Who y'all be with?" they asked, wanting to know our gang affiliation. "What'cha ridin'?"

"We ain't nothin'," Paul replied. "We're not about that. We're just hanging at the party. Havin' a good time."

Then one of the GDs spotted Paul's earrings. Even though Paul had a skullcap pulled over his left ear, the earrings could be seen glistening from the street light. The GD reached toward Paul to try to pull up his cap.

Paul slapped his hand down and warned, "Don't you be touchin' me! Do you know who I am?"

When gang members say "Do you know who I am?" they mean, "Do you know who you're messin' with? Do you know I have a reputation as a badass, as someone you better not fuck with?"

Before the GD could respond, Paul lunged forward, faking like he was going to hit him. At the same time, he yelled, "Break!"

As we'd agreed, Paul, David, George, and I took off running, but Opie stayed behind and threw a punch at one of the GDs, hitting him squarely in the face.

I ran fast, with several GDs just behind me. I ducked as one of them swung his arms to try to hit me in the head. All of a sudden, the GD stopped, turned, and went back. I swiveled around and saw Opie lying on the ground. Several GDs were stomping him!

By the time the four of us got back to help Opie, the GDs had run off. Opie's face was swollen and bleeding. The GDs had stolen his athletic bag, which had a pair of shoes and some clothes in it.

"Fuck them pussies!" Paul said. "We're gonna get your shit back."

I don't know what we were thinking, but we walked in the direction of the GDs, yelling to get their attention. We found them a block away beating another boy in the middle of the street.

Paul picked up an empty glass bottle from the ground. He broke it on the pavement to make a sharp edge and waved it in the air yelling, "Punks! Y'all ain't shit. Come down here and we'll whup your asses!"

The GDs ran off down the street again. "Let it go," Opie said. "They can have the fuckin' bag."

We continued walking toward the El station and climbed the stairs up to the platform to wait for the train. We found a bunch of people, including some other VLs, mingling there. Then some GDs came onto the platform. We were trapped. One of them shouted, "There goes those motherfuckers right there!" They charged toward us. Everyone was throwing punches. Some of the VLs jumped down on the train track and fled. Paul told us to stay put as he took off and ran down the platform, drawing some GDs with him. When the El arrived, everyone was yelling and screaming as they tried to get on board. Opie, George, and I hopped onto the train, narrowly escaping to safety. During the commotion, we'd gotten separated from David. We didn't know what happened to him.

We decided to go to George's grandmother's house, the closest place of refuge, and stay the night. Opie and I called our mother around 4:00 a.m. and told her that we'd missed the last bus and didn't want to walk home. She told us that she had awakened in the middle of the night; the Lord had come to her in a dream. She sensed that something was wrong, but we told her that we were all right.

The next day we found out what had happened to our friends. Paul had been trapped on the lower level of the El platform. David heard him scream and ran down to help. He managed to stop the GDs from throwing Paul off the platform, but both Paul and David were beaten badly, with knife wounds in their stomachs. The GDs left them for dead as they ran off. If it were not for the cold weather, Paul and David might have died. They had lost a lot of blood, and the doctors said that the cold had slowed the bleeding and probably saved their lives.

I visited David in the hospital. I couldn't look at his face; it was a mess. I felt responsible for what had happened. We should have all gone down together, I thought. Now there was no turning back. I started feeling hatred toward the GDs. This is when I became committed to fighting for *my* gang.

When I first became involved with gangs, few members were carrying guns. A broken bottle or knife, a baseball bat, or golf club were the weapons of choice. Dobby always carried golf clubs in the trunk of his car. If the cops stopped us, we could tell them that we were going to hit some balls at the driving range. But if we had an opportunity to get into a fight, we could pop the trunk, pull out the clubs, and get it on.

Still, in those days gang fighting was mostly a matter of fists, or perhaps some karate kicks for those of us who knew a little of the martial arts. I had taken lessons for a while, though I didn't stick with it. I didn't like the fact that in order to get promoted to the next belt level, you had to fight someone in the higher classification. One of my friends in the class had gotten his butt kicked. I thought, "I don't need this shit." But I kept practicing on my own, and the skills came in handy on the street. I also got stronger by lifting weights.

Although I occasionally drank and smoked marijuana with my friends before we went to a party, getting high didn't really appeal to me. My friends would jump around and act silly, but I liked to keep my wits about me. I was worried about getting trapped somewhere with a bunch of GDs and not being prepared to fight. My role was to chaperone my friends, make sure they didn't do anything stupid, and back them up if they got into trouble.

Kim was the one who most often instigated the fights. When he arrived at a party, he'd strut onto the dance floor and start dancing and throwing up gang signs, disrespecting members of other gangs. I'd be standing in a corner, talking to a girl—which was the main reason I went to these parties—and someone would approach me and ask, "Ain't that your boy out there?" And sure enough, Kim would be pushing and shoving somebody. But Kim wasn't a very good fighter, so I'd have to step in and clean up his mess.

I'd get angry at Kim for all the trouble he caused: "Why do you always have to do the same old shit? I ain't gonna keep hanging with your ass if all you want to do is fight."

"Fuck you, man," Kim replied. "You do the same shit."

The truth is that I didn't really mind Kim starting all those fights because I enjoyed beating up the GDs, but some of our friends were getting tired of the fistfighting. They wanted to escalate the warfare. Duane, a thin youth who didn't like to fistfight, was obsessed with getting a gun. That's all he ever talked about: "Why are we fighting these same motherfuckers all the time? We need to start putting a bullet in their motherfuckin' asses."

"Fuck that. They're not worth the price of the bullets," I told them, hoping they'd chill out. I had as much hatred for the GDs as any of them. But I didn't want to kill anybody.

My cousin Larry, as usual, didn't help matters. Larry and Kim had been getting into it with Bobby Brooks, a rival GD. The hostility got even more intense when Larry began dating one of Bobby's girlfriends. Larry and Kim threatened to shoot Bobby. I tried to cool them down: "He ain't worth it. You want to go to jail? Spend the rest of your life in prison?"

"Fuck that Boonie!" Kim exclaimed. "Bobby and them niggas tried to jump me on the bus. When I was with my mother! We need to kill that motherfucker!"

One night Kim got into a fight with Bobby outside of Mr. T's restaurant. Larry came out of the restaurant, jumped in, and beat up Bobby pretty badly. At the time, Bobby may have thought that it was me, not Larry, who had done it. Larry and I looked alike, and I often let him wear my high-school football jacket. Bobby also knew that Kim and I were best friends and always hung out together. It was inevitable that he'd try to get revenge.

About a week later, Kim and I saw Bobby walking down the street. We slipped between two houses and waited for him to pass. Kim was packing a gun and wanted to shoot Bobby. But I grabbed the gun and stopped him. Bobby didn't see us and never knew how close he came to getting killed.

During the whole time we were involved in gangs, with all the violence that occurred, we rarely thought about or had contact with the police. If you beat someone else in a fight, no one ever called the police about you. And if you lost a fight, all you thought about was rounding up your friends to retaliate.

There are few incidents with the police during my youth that stick out in my mind. I remember when I was just six or seven years old, Opie and I got caught shoplifting Easter bunny candy from a local grocery store. The storeowner threatened to call the cops and send us to jail. I was crying and blamed Opie for making me do it. The storeowner let us go.

Then there was the time that Maurice and I got caught throwing rocks at cars. It was something that we did for laughs. This time we hit an unmarked police car. As the detectives stopped the car, we tried to run away. They chased us down and corralled us into the backseat of the vehicle. They asked us where we lived and drove us home. After talking to my mother, they decided this was a good opportunity to teach Maurice and me a lesson. The detectives took us down to the station for several hours. One of the detectives gave us a tour and explained what would happen if we got into any more trouble. We might never see our parents again, he said. The whole experience scared me a great deal, and I thought I never wanted to see the inside of a jail again.

When I was older and got involved in gangs, however, the police were the last thing on my mind. If anything, I was defiant toward them, especially if I knew they couldn't pin anything on me. In my neighborhood, most people distrusted the police—and other white people in authority—and felt that they abused their power and harassed us for no reason.

On one occasion, when my friends and I were walking home from a football game, somebody shouted, "Here come the cops! Here come the cops!" Just as the squad car pulled up beside us, I hollered, "Fuck them, we're not doing anything wrong!" A white cop was driving the car and a black cop, who overheard this remark, was on the passenger's side of the vehicle. As I began walking away with my friends, the black cop leaned out the window and yelled, "Hey, boy, bring your black ass back here!" I kept walking, which caused the cop to exclaim, "You heard me, motherfucker! You ain't gonna stop?"

At that point, I decided I better stop. I turned around and pointed at myself as if to say I hadn't realized he'd been talking to me. "Yeah, you. Come over here," he commanded. I walked over to the car and he said, "What did you say before? I heard you say 'fuck you.' You can't say 'fuck you' to the police."

"Okay, whatever," I said dismissively.

This made the cop even angrier. He got out of the car and noticed a black handle that was sticking out of my coat pocket. It was only a hairbrush, but he thought it was a gun. As he reached forward to take it, I pushed his hand away. Then he grabbed me and slammed me up against the car. The cop searched me, as his partner, who was now out of the car, too, told my friends to "get out of here."

"Where do you live?" the cop demanded.

"Around the corner," I replied.

"Tell me where you live."

"Down the street, around the corner. . . . You just think you're tough because you've got a badge."

"You little punk. I'll whup your ass."

"Well, take off your gun."

With that remark, I'd frustrated him so much that he simply waved at me in disgust and told me to "go home." As I walked off, the cops followed me for a while in their patrol car, but I cut through an alley and lost them.

4. The Shooting

pril 16, 1986, started off like any other day. Little did I know it would turn out to be a day I'd never forget. When I arrived at Chicago Vocational High School that morning, one of my classmates told me that she'd had a premonition of some ominous event that awaited me. "You need to slow down," Annette warned. "I had a dream that something bad is going to happen to you."

"You dreamed about me?" I teased. "Was it kinky? You want to hook up with me?"

"No, seriously. You need to slow down."

Annette was right. I was stressed out. I'd been getting into it with the Gangster Disciples that entire week at school. GDs who didn't even attend CVS were coming by and calling my friends and me out to fight.

On my way home from school that day, Ricky Young and I were riding the bus home from school. We were sitting in the back, trying to mind our own business, when some GD started taunting Ricky about "whupping his ass."

At first, I wasn't paying any attention to what was going on. But Ricky, who had a short temper, began arguing with him. That's when I looked over at the GD, and he said, "Yeah, you get a good look motherfucker, because after I whup *his* punk ass, I'm going to whup *your* ass, too." I thought to myself, "What is this shit? You don't even know me."

There were other GDs and Vice Lords on the bus with us. One of the VLs said, "Fuck 'em. Let's get off at State Street and whup their asses. Let's handle our business." Neither Ricky nor I needed much encouragement to fight—that's probably why we got along so well—so we thought we'd go with them.

At the State Street stop, a few GDs and VLs got off of the bus, but Annette and her friends held Ricky and me back, pleading with us not to go. As the bus drove off, Ricky and I saw that someone had hit our friend, John, with some kind of pole, probably a baseball bat. It looked like John was hurt pretty badly. Ricky and I pulled the cord to get the bus driver to let us off, but he wouldn't stop. I was steaming with anger. An older VL who had remained on the bus told us, "Y'all was smart not to get off. Y'all didn't need to go through *that*."

When I got home my mother told me, "Boonie, you shouldn't be going outside anymore today. Hang low. There's evil spirits in the air." It was around the time that the United States had been bombing military installations in Libya in retaliation against Muammar Qadhafi for sponsoring terrorism. "We done bombed Qadhafi," my mother said. "Satan is on a rampage."

Later that afternoon, I was watching television when Kim came over and suggested we go to the game room, the neighborhood arcade. When we got to the game room, the place was packed. A few GDs from the neighborhood were there, but these particular youths respected my reputation and usually left me alone.

I was sitting on a bench beneath a big bay window, with Kim sitting to my right, and a girlfriend, Stacey, to my left. I had my head bowed, absorbed in my thoughts, contemplating what had happened the past week and strategizing about how I was going to retaliate against my enemies. Unbeknownst to me, Bobby Brooks walked into the game room with Maurice (not my brother), a guy I'd never seen before. Bobby flashed a twenty-two caliber handgun at the other GDs and motioned for them to clear the room.

I still had my head down and wasn't aware of what was happening as Bobby and Maurice approached me. Maurice put on a pair of gloves and asked Bobby, "Is that him, right there?" Bobby, who never actually saw my face, said, "Yeah, that's him."

Kim and Stacey were thinking, "What's wrong with Boonie?" Normally, I would've never tolerated anyone standing so close to me. I would've said "What the fuck are you doing?" and immediately challenged them to a fight.

Suddenly, Maurice hit me on the side of my head with his fist. I was momentarily stunned. I couldn't believe that someone would do something like that *in my own neighborhood.* Immediately I jumped up and punched Maurice several times in the face as he stumbled backward. Adrenaline was flowing through my body. All my anger about what had transpired the past week was directed at Maurice. I wanted to kill him.

Meanwhile Kim had jumped up, too, but Bobby put his gun in his face and told him to "get back." I didn't see the gun and charged toward Maurice, hitting him several more times. Maurice yelled, "Get the missile out! Get the missile out! Shoot 'im! Shoot 'im!"

All of a sudden I heard a loud bang! Bobby, who was standing just seven feet away, had shot me from behind in the lower part of my back. At first, I didn't realize I'd been shot, but then I felt a burning sensation in my back and a tingling, numbing sensation in my legs. As I turned around to see where the noise came from, my legs gave out. Maurice caught me as I was falling and laid me on the floor. Then a second gunshot went off. I thought they'd shot Kim. My heart cringed with fear; I was more worried about him than me.

But Kim wasn't shot. He'd run out of the game room to get help and had found Opie at the house: "Man, they got Boonie! They got Boonie! He's trapped in the game room! I think he's been shot!"

I was lying on the floor in the game room. All I could see was Larry Jackson, a GD from the neighborhood. Larry and I had grown up together, but we'd ended up in rival gangs and no longer spoke to each other. Larry was crying hysterically, shocked at what had happened: "Man, Boonie, I'm sorry. I didn't know what was going down." He wanted to pick me up and move me.

"Don't touch me, Larry! Don't touch me!" I insisted. I had learned first aid and knew you weren't supposed to move an injured person.

"Come on, Boonie, don't be that way," Larry pleaded.

"Don't touch me. Just get away from me," I repeated.

During the fight, we had knocked over the gas radiator that was in the room. I could smell the leaking fumes. I thought I was going to suffocate and die. I felt exhausted. My eyes were getting heavy. I looked down at my legs. They were lying straight out, but it felt like they were bent at the knees. It was the last sensation I ever felt in my legs.

Finally, the ambulance arrived. A female paramedic came into the game room and asked me a bunch of questions about what had happened. I answered her calmly and told her I couldn't feel my legs. She pulled a pair of scissors out of her bag and started cutting into the pant legs on my favorite pants, gray baggies with pockets on the side. "Hey, don't cut my pants," I complained. "We have to," she said, poking me with a needle. But I couldn't feel a thing.

"Are you gonna take me to the hospital?" I asked, feeling cold and tired. "I just wanna sleep."

"You have to keep talking," she said.

Another paramedic came into the room. He spoke briefly with his partner and asked me the same questions. "Why are you doing this?" I said. "She wrote it down. Get it from her."

Then my mother came into the room. Up to that point, she hadn't known about my gang activity. She just looked at me and said, "Boonie, there's nothing we can do for you. You're in the Lord's hands now." With that, she just left.

The paramedics kept working on me, and I was frustrated because it was taking so long to get moving. Finally, they got me onto a stretcher and took me outside to the ambulance. I looked around to see who was there. Everyone was upset about what had happened. I remember feeling glad that the girls were crying over me. At the time, I didn't know who had shot me, but I knew that my friends would find out and retaliate.

I was first taken to St. Bernard Hospital, one of the worst medical facilities in the area. The paramedics rolled me into the emergency department. "He's a gunshot victim. Got shot in the back," one of them told the attending physician. I was actually surprised to hear this because, due to the small size of the bullet, I hadn't lost a lot of blood and wasn't fully aware of how badly I was hurt. "We better get him over to Northwestern," the doctor said.

The paramedics took me to Northwestern Memorial Hospital in downtown Chicago. By that time, I was experiencing a lot of pain in my stomach. The doctors told me they were going to have to do some exploratory surgery to see what kind of internal damage I had sustained. The last thing I remember was the nurse placing a gas mask over my face. For a moment, I lay there, rambling, "Man, this shit isn't gonna work. I've just been shot. I'm gonna need some drugs."

The surgeon cut me open with an incision from the top of my sternum to my naval. The bullet had ricocheted inside my body and lodged in my tailbone. Although my spinal cord was not severed, the impact of the bullet had inflamed the muscles around my spine and damaged the nerves around it. The doctors decided against surgically removing the bullet, fearing that would cause more harm than leaving it in. Otherwise, there appeared to be no further internal complications.

When I woke up after the surgery, I found myself strapped to a flat bed, with a tube in my nose, several IVs in my arm, a catheter attached to my penis, and surgical staples holding my torso together. I was extremely drowsy, too drugged to realize the extent of my injury or how it would change my life. My mother, father, brothers, Kim, and Dobby were standing around my bed in the intensive care unit. I could tell they were all nervous. Dobby held onto the bed; I could feel it shaking. My mother told him, "Step back. Don't touch the bed." Kim was angry and upset: "Boonie, if you had let me shoot Bobby a long time ago, this shit wouldn't have happened." But I didn't feel much like talking and soon fell back into a deep sleep.

The first night in the hospital, after everyone had left, felt like the longest night of my life. I couldn't move, and I drifted in and out of consciousness, still dazed from the drugs I'd been given during surgery. I wanted to sleep and never wake up. A nurse came by every four hours to turn me over. Awake, I looked over at the heart monitor and watched my pulse go up and down. When my pulse got low, I thought I was going to die. Previously I'd had premonitions about not living to see my twenty-first birthday; that was the nature of the life I'd been living. I worried that this premonition was coming true. Then the monitor would start beeping and get higher. I thought it was responding to my emotions, and I eventually learned to control my pulse, to make the monitor go up and down at will.

I was kept bedridden in intensive care for nine days. Everyone, including the doctors, was uncertain about what was going to happen to me, even if I would live or die. I wasn't allowed to eat any solid food. The only nourishment that I received was pumped through my nose from a feeding tube, which I could feel in the back of my throat. It was very uncomfortable, even painful. When my godsister, Nancy Mauldin, came to visit, she sneaked me some sour cream and onion potato chips. Although I couldn't eat them, I savored the taste of the salted chips touching my tongue.

I kept the television on, but didn't really watch anything. I just wanted some background noise to drown out the droning of the medical equipment that was running all the time. I wasn't able to talk much. The only thing I looked forward to was my parents coming to visit every day around 6:00 p.m.

The doctors were uncertain about my prognosis for walking. On the one hand, they said I might never be able to walk again, that I'd need to use a wheelchair to get around. On the other hand, they said there was a possibility that the bullet, over time, might dislodge on its own. In that case, they could go back in and take it out, and my chances of walking would improve. Thus, at first I didn't fully grasp the permanency of my condition. My mother, in particular, remained hopeful that I might walk again one day.

After my time in intensive care, I was transferred to another hospital room. Gradually the nurses had me sit up in the bed, beginning at a thirty-five-degree angle. The first time I tried to sit up, I got sick and vomited and almost passed out.

I was bored to death in the hospital. When the nurses came in, they would make small talk while they were performing their tasks, but there was absolutely nothing to do. There was little on television that was of interest to me, and I didn't feel like reading. So I just laid there and looked out the window, waiting for someone to visit. The doctors thought I was depressed and sent a psychiatrist to see me. The psychiatrist talked to me for a couple of hours. "There is nothing wrong with him," he explained to the other doctors. "What do you expect from the kid? There's nobody here to talk to, nothing for him to do."

I learned from Opie and my friends that Bobby, the guy who'd shot me, had been arrested. As Bobby was running out of the game room, the owner had grabbed a gun and fired at him through the window. Bobby was hit in the shoulder and taken to the hospital, but the gunshot wound caused him no lasting injuries.

Everyone wanted payback against the despised GDs. There were certain people in our group, like me, who were simply off limits; if you messed with one of us, you could expect a massive retaliatory response. Before, Opie and I had tried to stop our friends from shooting the GDs; we had wanted to hurt them—beat them up—but not kill them. Now everything had changed. Opie wanted to call for a nationwide move-out against them. This meant rounding up all our allies, driving around the neighborhood, and shooting all the GDs they could find. I told Opie that was just fine with me.

Kathy Parnell, the choir director from our church, had spoken to Opie about this. She knew the mentality of gang members and wanted to prevent an all-out war. Opie refused to listen to her, so she came to the hospital to talk to me.

"You know, Boonie," she said. "I stopped by your house and talked to Opie. Everyone's all pissed off. They're ready to start going around and shooting up the city."

"Bobby fucked up," I mumbled dismissively. "He shouldn't have shot me."

"So what's gonna happen now?" Kathy asked.

"Whatever happens, happens."

"Y'all gonna go out and shoot some of them? And they gonna come back and shoot some of your friends. What's going to change? You're still gonna be in this hospital. You're still gonna be in a wheelchair. What's it gonna solve? What's it gonna prove?"

"It's gonna prove that they shouldn't have shot me."

"Well, at least you're alive. What happens if one of your brothers, one of your friends, gets killed? What if some innocent kid gets shot down? You can stop that from happening."

"Naw, I ain't gonna stop them from doing anything."

"Think about it, Boonie. Think about doing what's right."

In spite of what I told Kathy, she had gotten through to me, and for the first time, I began questioning the wild and reckless lifestyle I'd been living. "This is stupid," I thought. "The people we're going to shoot really didn't have anything to do with me getting shot." Besides, I'd learned that the shooting had been a case of mistaken identity; Bobby had confused me with my cousin Larry.

I decided to tell Opie to call off the move-out, but I was worried he wouldn't listen to me. He'd think I was punking out and do it anyway.

I called Opie on the phone: "Hey, man, I want you to call it off."

"For what?" asked Opie. "I got everybody ready. Foster Park is coming through. Rock Island. Stone Terrace. They're waiting for me to give the word. Why do you want me to call it off?"

"'Cause I want to be there when it happens," I explained, thinking I'd found a way for everyone to save face, at least for awhile.

Opie hesitated as he considered my request: "All right, I'll tell them you don't want nothin' done till you get out."

Everyone respected my wishes, but the anticipation only heightened their resolve. They would say things like "Man, when Boonie comes home, we're gonna tear it up. We're gonna get some payback." Nonetheless, I hoped that by the time I got home from the hospital, they would all cool down. In my neighborhood, however, a grudge was not something easily forgotten.

Part II **Transitions**

5. Road to Recovery

During my first month at Northwestern Memorial Hospital, I lost a lot of weight. I was shocked the first time I saw myself in a mirror; I didn't recognize the person looking back at me. My muscles had atrophied, and my entire body looked so skinny. I had to wear stockings on my legs to keep the blood circulating, and I received blood-thinner injections to prevent clotting. The physical therapists worked on my range of motion and eventually got me to sit upright in bed without feeling nauseated. Then I was transferred to the Rehabilitation Institute of Chicago (RIC), which was connected to Northwestern Memorial by an underground tunnel. RIC is one of the best rehab clinics in the area. Fortunately, my father had good medical coverage through his job at Ford Motor Company. If it were not for that coverage, I would have been sent to a county hospital and probably wouldn't have received the quality of care that was available at RIC.

At RIC, I started using a wheelchair. The therapists worked me into it gradually, an hour or so at a time. That's when it hit me that in spite of the doctors' equivocation I'd probably have to use a chair for the *rest of my life.* It was a reality check, and I was scared to death. I'd gone from being a confident gang member who loved to freely roam the streets to being a patient who was dependent on the RIC nursing staff for all my basic needs. I had lost control of my bladder and had to learn to use a catheter to urinate. I needed help bathing, getting dressed, and transferring in and out of my chair. The staff was always busy, and sometimes I'd have to wait a long time for assistance. If I got tired during the day and wanted to lay down to rest, it could take as much as an hour before someone would come by to help me transfer from my chair to my bed. I felt like a little child, and I hated it. I realized that I would have to learn all the little things I had once taken for granted all over again.

It would have been easy for me to give up at that time, and today when I tell people my story, they often assume that I must have fallen into a deep depression. But this is not what happened because I decided early on that I wasn't going to give in to self-pity or despair. I remembered how my friends and I had reacted to James, a neighborhood youth with muscular dystrophy, who was the first person I'd ever known who had a disability. Although James used a power wheelchair, we all tried to include him in everything we did. We even changed the rules for touch football to accommodate him; if the passer hit James with the ball, it was counted as a catch. But James would at times feel sorry for himself, and some of the kids began to tire of his negative attitude. Eventually, when we made plans to do something, someone would inevitably ask, "What about James?" Someone else would reply, "Naw, forget about him."

I was determined not to end up like James. Besides, all my friends still looked up to me and I needed to be strong for *them.* There is only one time I remember feeling genuinely depressed. I hadn't seen my friends since the first night after I was shot. My mother brought Kim and a couple of the guys to RIC to see me. I was sitting in my bed waiting for them to arrive, and all of a sudden, I felt really sad, but then I thought, "What am I doing? I can't let them see me like this." So I put a smile on my face and decided not to let myself feel that way again. People have told me that I must have been in denial, but I see things differently, as I tried to make the best of my new situation. Later, I would even say that my gunshot injury was both the worst and best thing that happened to me: If I hadn't been shot, I would've probably ended up in prison or been killed, like so many of my former gang associates.

In some ways, I think my religious background had something to do with my positive adjustment. It's not that I believed, like my mother, that my fate was in God's hands, nor did I think there was some broader spiritual significance to what had happened. It's just that in church, we'd been taught to accept the things that happened to people (including illness and death) and not mire in regret about what might have been. I had always lived my life one day at a time. So now I realized that what I needed to do was focus on my physical condition, learn how my new body worked, and do whatever it took to make it work better.

At RIC, my therapeutic boot camp, I began a full regimen of physical and occupational therapy. I continued working on my range of motion and started lifting light weights. I even learned to walk with braces, although I relied on a wheelchair to get around. I became increasingly skilled at transferring in and out of my chair and at maneuvering it to get where I wanted to go. The work was hard, grueling at times, but I could see that I was making a lot of progress.

Each morning I lay in bed until a nurse came in to help me get ready for my daily routine. One day a new nurse walked into my room. Her name was Gladys, a crotchety, straight-talking woman in her mid-thirties. When Gladys saw me sitting on the bed in my sleeping gown, she said, "I'm not getting your grown ass dressed. You dress your own damn self."

My hospital wardrobe consisted of jogging suits, for the staff didn't want me to wear jeans or anything with pockets because of skin problems that might develop from rubbing on the chair. Besides, jogging outfits were easier to put on. "I can dress my damn self," I told Gladys. "I don't need your help."

From that point on, I got dressed on my own. It might've taken me an hour to get ready, but I did it. Gladys was proud of me, and I was proud too. For a while, however, I still needed help with bathing, and I remember one incident very well. Gladys was giving me a shower, and for the first time since my accident I got an erection. I looked up at Gladys and gave her a big smile. "Don't you be looking at me like that," she said, and she threw the towel at me and walked out of the room.

I was happy when I realized I could still have an erection. And it was more than an involuntary response, for my spinal-cord injury was, in medical parlance, "incomplete." I still had use of my hip muscles and felt sensation through my lower buttocks, but no one ever talked to me about the possibility of having sex, about what I could expect of my new life as a person with a disability. Later I learned that although I could reach a sexual climax and experience a sense of release, I was unable to ejaculate. At the same time, I also became less self-centered than I'd been in the past and learned to be more in tune with what my partner was feeling, to experience orgasm through her.

During my time at RIC, I also met other youths who were gunshot victims, other gang members who were the casualties of Chicago's inner-city warfare. In the hospital, however, our gang affiliation didn't seem to matter much. We were all in the same boat, all trying to learn how to live with a disabling condition. It was somewhat consoling to know that I wasn't the only one going through this ordeal. It helped me overcome any feeling of isolation that threatened to creep up on me.

One day I was sitting in the RIC lobby when another young patient pushed by me in a wheelchair, popped a wheelie, and took off. I thought it would be really cool to be able to do that. Everyone would be impressed if I could pop a wheelie and do tricks in my chair. I started to think that if I was going to be in a wheelchair, I wanted to get really good at using it. Soon I learned how to find my center of gravity in my chair and pop wheelies like the guy I saw in the lobby.

Overall, I recall my time at RIC as a positive experience. The nurses and rehab staff were very supportive and helpful. In addition to the physical exercises, they taught me practical daily living skills, like remembering to call in advance before going out to a restaurant or movie theatre to make sure it was wheelchair accessible. I also learned how to drive a car with hand controls (which are connected to the gas and brake pedals). After practicing on a simulated machine, I was thrilled when I got to take a vehicle out for a spin on Lakeshore Drive.

By early June, nearly two months after I was shot, I was ready to be released from the inpatient program at RIC, but first our home had to be evaluated for accessibility. Two of my therapists went with me on a home visit. They made sure my bedroom was set up properly, showed me how to transfer in and out of my chair in the bathroom, and generally prepared me for all the little things I needed to look out for when I went home for good.

After that, I received a weekend pass to see how I would do on my own. I was a little apprehensive about this, excited but nervous. What if something went wrong? I wouldn't have the RIC staff to help me. My family was apprehensive, too, and my friends weren't sure how to react. I felt like a stranger in my own home.

My mother tried to pamper me, wanting to help me get dressed and do everything for me. If she'd see me reaching for something, she'd say, "I'll get that for you. Save your strength." I could see that she felt a need to take care of me and that she was much more sympathetic than my father. He simply said, "See what all this gang shit gets you." I didn't want to hear this, but I didn't want help from my mother either.

My friends' reactions varied. Some stayed away altogether, while others hung around the house telling me they couldn't imagine what they would do if something like that happened to them. They weren't sure how to react around me. Some of them acted like my mother, wanting to do things for me, but I told them I could do them myself. Eventually they said, "Man, Boonie's still the same." Then if I asked them for help, they said, "To hell with you. Do it yourself." I think that was a defining moment for me, when everyone realized that I was the same person I'd always been; it's just that instead of walking, I now used a wheelchair to get around.

About a week before I was discharged from RIC, I was hanging around the hospital lobby. Bob Trotter, the therapeutic recreation coordinator at RIC, happened to pass by. Bob had contracted polio as a youth, and although he was able to walk, he used a wheelchair for mobility. Bob played for the men's wheelchair basketball team that was sponsored by RIC, and he also coached the RIC juniors' team. After introducing himself, he asked whether I'd like to play with the juniors. "Sure, if it'll get me out of this hospital," I replied.

The idea of playing basketball in a wheelchair brought back memories of Earl Jordan, a kid I'd occasionally seen shooting baskets on the outdoor court at Alonzo Stagg. At the time, I'd thought it was cool that someone who used a wheelchair could actually play ball. I'd spoken to Earl a few times and rebounded some shots for him before going off to play with my able-bodied friends. I never could've imagined that one day *I* would be playing basketball in a chair, too.

Bob arranged for a van to take me to a game, which was held at a nearby downtown gym. That's when I met the other players on the team, guys like Jorge Alforo, Eric Barber, and, coincidentally, Earl Jordan. While I used a conventional hospital chair, they all pushed lightweight sports chairs. When Bob put me in the game, I trailed behind the others the entire time. My chair was heavier and I wasn't in as good condition. By the time I got to one end of the court, the shot had already been taken and everyone else was heading the other way.

No one would pass me the ball. When Jorge finally did, I threw up a shot as I fell backward in my chair. Miraculously the ball went in!

I was pumped, but unfortunately I had to leave the game early because RIC had a 9:00 p.m. curfew for inpatients. That night, as I lay in bed, my mind was racing about the prospects of playing competitive sports again. The guys on the team were so full of life, unlike many of the youths I'd met at RIC. It had made me feel good just to be around them, to have peers who, by their example, showed me that a disability didn't have to stop me from leading a physically active life.

The next day Bob came by to see me and told me that RIC had won the game in double overtime. Then he said, "You know, you played pretty good for a beginner. I bet if I got you a sports chair you'd play even better."

"That would be great!" I said excitedly.

Later, Bob returned with a lightweight sports chair, which he said I could borrow for a week but which I kept for a longer time. I started pushing myself around in my new chair. "Man, how'd you get that chair?" the other patients asked enviously.

"I'm on the basketball team," I said proudly.

When I first got involved in wheelchair basketball, I had no idea of the rich history of the game. It began in 1946, when disabled World War II veterans played pick-up games during their stays at Veterans Administration (VA) hospitals. Two years later, the Paralyzed Veterans of America began sponsoring several organized teams, and the Birmingham Flying Wheels (from California) made the first of several cross-country tours, competing around the country and spreading the word about the sport. An immediate result was the formation of the first non-VA team, the Kansas City Wheelchair Bulldozers, later called the Rolling Pioneers.[1]

Around that time, Timothy Nugent, director of student rehabilitation services at the University of Illinois at Galesburg, established the first collegiate team. Although the state of Illinois soon closed its

Galesburg campus, Nugent started a team at the University of Illinois at Urbana-Champaign, the university that developed the prototype for disabled student services around the country.

Nugent also organized the first National Wheelchair Basketball Tournament, which was held in Galesburg in 1949.[2] During that tournament, the participating athletes decided to organize the National Wheelchair Basketball Association (NWBA), the sport's first national governing body. Nugent served as its technical adviser and commissioner for the next twenty-five years. The NWBA's mission included working on the standardization of rules, determining the eligibility of participating individuals and teams, conducting tournament competitions, and "foster[ing] the concept of the participant as an athlete in his own right, and by doing so, establish[ing] the validity of the sport as a legitimate avenue of athletic expression for all disabled individuals."[3]

Soon, players began experimenting with the design of their chairs, removing the armrests and push handles and lowering the backrest to eliminate unnecessary bulk and weight. They attached antitip casters to the underside of the rear frame, several inches off the ground; if the front end of the chair lifted off the floor, the casters prevented it from tipping over. The players also angled the wheels, making them farther apart at the bottom than at the top, giving the chairs more stability and making them easier to turn. By the late 1960s, the manufacture of tubular stainless steel chairs lowered the standard weight from about fifty to thirty to thirty-five pounds.[4]

The contemporary lightweight sports wheelchair, however, was apparently the brainchild of Marilyn Hamilton, who became a paraplegic after suffering a spinal-cord injury in a hang-gliding accident in 1978. Prior to her injury, Hamilton had been an avid tennis player. She found the conventional hospital chairs, even the stainless steel models, too heavy and bulky for tennis. She asked two of her hang-glider friends, who designed gliders, to build her a lighter chair. The twenty-six pound aluminum chair they came up with was light and sturdy. It had a sleek and sporty look, with a low-slung back and compact frame that resembled a multispeed racing bicycle. Hamilton and her friends started their own business, manufacturing and selling their Quickie brand wheelchairs as fast as they could. The chairs came in a variety of colors and transformed an unappealing medical apparatus into a symbol of fun, sport, and disability pride. After my release from RIC, my parents bought one of these cool sports chairs for me.[5]

I was formally discharged from RIC on June 16, 1986. The adjustment back home was a gradual process, but things went fairly well overall. When the fall semester rolled around, the Chicago public-school officials wouldn't let me finish my senior year at Chicago Vocational High School. Instead, they made me enroll in Spaulding High School, the place where they segregated all the students with disabilities.

I was very unhappy at Spaulding, which enrolled students with both physical and cognitive impairments. Some of the kids in my classes just stared into space and drooled; they didn't seem capable of learning anything. I was treated like someone who was mentally disabled, but there was nothing wrong with my mind. I just couldn't get around without a wheelchair.

There were a lot of physically disabled girls at the school who liked me, but I wasn't interested in them. They complained that I was conceited and that I thought I was too good to date girls who used wheelchairs. In my mind, however, it had nothing to do with their chairs. I just wasn't attracted to them. Besides, at the time I wasn't ready to deal with a relationship with the opposite sex.

While I was enrolled at Spaulding, I continued to play with the RIC juniors' basketball team. At first, my work habits—my commitment to the game—left something to be desired. I arrived late for practices and games dressed in a nice pair of pants and shirt rather than in athletic attire; I had gotten rid of all my sweats after I came home from RIC. The other guys started calling me GQ, after the *Gentleman's Quarterly* fashion magazine. Still, I was falling in love with the game. It was pure fun, and it was good for my self-esteem. It made me feel proud and confident and increased my sense of control over my body. I also relished the camaraderie and approval of my new teammates, who taught me a lot about living with a disability; even for things I learned in therapy, they showed me an easier way to do them.

The guys on the RIC team were quite serious about excelling at wheelchair basketball. They considered themselves athletes, practiced all the time, and worked hard to become better players. On the other hand, the players at Spaulding High School, which had its own team, were just interested in having a little fun and recreation. They played in hospital wheelchairs, not sports chairs, and even left their backpacks and cup holders on their chairs during practices and games. They didn't work out, and most of them weren't strong enough to get the ball up to the basket. They often threw up air balls, which landed on their heads, making them look silly. They didn't know how to pass or dribble the ball, and they had no desire to learn the basic skills of the game.

According to the rules of wheelchair basketball, a player may take two pushes with the ball in his lap before being required to dribble. Once he dribbles the ball, he can return it to his lap and start the sequence over again. This deceptively simple maneuver takes a good deal of practice to master. When I first started playing, I had trouble keeping the ball in front of me. It continually drifted behind my chair, and I didn't know how to stop and turn around to get it.

Since I had trouble dribbling the ball, Bob Trotter thought I was better suited for the center or forward position. He was constantly yelling at me to "get down the court." But I wanted to be a guard, a ball handler, and I often pleaded with my teammates to give me the ball so I could dribble it. They rarely did, because they were worried that Bob would take them out of the game.

I must admit that, back then, my RIC teammates and I had a rather snobbish attitude toward the weaker Spaulding players. One might assume that people with disabilities all feel empathy toward each other, but this is not necessarily the case. Although disability rights activists have tried to develop a united front to advance a political cause, this has been a strategic alliance that masks some rather diverse impairments and attitudes among those of us who are disabled. Indeed, I was reluctant to associate myself with the Spaulding players for fear of being ridiculed by my RIC peers.

There was only one time when I actually played in a game with the Spaulding team. The team was short a player for a game against Illinois Children's Hospital, and I agreed to go along. John Koffey, the Spaulding guidance counselor, who was a quadriplegic, was the coach. Koffey told me, "Melvin, you're *not* here to shoot. You're here to make the other players look good, to make sure they get involved."

I was rather annoyed at this and thought, "Okay then, I'm not going to shoot at all." But after not taking a shot for the entire first half, I looked up at the scoreboard and saw that our team was down 22–0. I thought, "We're getting our butts kicked. If we lose, I'll never hear the end of it from the RIC guys."

I started putting up one shot after another and brought the team to within one point with just seconds left in the game. Koffey called a time-out and said, "Okay, we're right in the game now. This is what we're gonna do. Melvin, I want you to inbound the ball. Pass it to Pritish. Pritish, you throw the ball up there as hard as you can. Give it your best."

Dismayed, I said, "What? I've scored all our points. Let me take the last shot."

"No," Koffey said. "Pritish, you're the man. You got to do this."

Reluctantly, I did what Koffey wanted and passed the ball to Pritish, who threw up an air ball. I got the rebound and missed a desperation shot that bounced off the front of the rim as time ran out. We lost the game.

When my RIC teammates heard about the loss, they teased me to no end. "Man, you played with Spaulding? How'd you let them lose? Y'all suck."

"I wasn't even trying hard," I told them. "I didn't start trying till the last ten minutes of the game. I scored all the points. But Koffey ass wouldn't let me take the last shot."

"He wouldn't let you shoot?" they said. "You should've shot anyway."

I just shook my head. I didn't mind the teasing; I enjoyed being with these guys. I knew that competitive athletics, like gang conflict, was not for the fainthearted. Humility was a trait I had yet to learn.

A turning point in my appreciation of wheelchair basketball occurred when Bob invited me to a men's tournament that was sponsored by RIC, where I watched more experienced and talented players. I was simply amazed when I saw the Chicago Sidewinders, one of the best teams in the country at the time. How quickly they propelled their chairs up and down the court as my head ping-ponged back and forth in disbelief. On a fast break, a player would throw a behind-the-back pass to a teammate who'd lay it up into the basket with an underhand scoop or over-the-head shot. They maneuvered their chairs so skillfully, stopping and pivoting on a dime and then shooting or passing the ball to the open man. It was at that moment that I knew what I wanted to do—to be as good as these men, to be like Mike, one of the best in the world. Later I would read about the legends of the game in *Sports 'N Spokes* magazine, the premier publication for disability sports. Watching and reading about these players opened up a whole new world for me.

In his motivational book, *Pushing Forward,* Randy Snow, whom I later played with on the 1996 U.S. wheelchair basketball team, writes of the power of dreams. Randy, who suffered a spinal-cord injury from a farming accident at age sixteen, is one of the most accomplished athletes in the history of wheelchair sports, excelling in tennis, track and field, and basketball. "Dreams," writes Randy, "make everyday life tolerable. . . . Without dreams life would be mediocre."[6]

Now I had a dream of my own. But I had yet to realize what this dream would entail, what revision of my mind-set I'd have to undergo, the hard work I'd have to invest in developing my basketball skills, in becoming a true student of the game. Still, the challenge appealed to me. After all, I had never backed away from a fight.

6. Breaking Away

Before my gunshot injury, I hadn't thought about going to college. I'd been majoring in cabinetmaking at Chicago Vocational High School and planned to join the army reserves upon graduation. Now that I was disabled, I knew that this game plan had to change.

I realized that a black man with a disability would have little chance of getting a decent job without a college degree. But when I discussed my college hopes with John Koffey, the Spaulding High School guidance counselor, he told me, "You don't need to go to school. You're just going to be disappointed. Why don't you collect social security and let the government take care of you?"

It was years later, after I had already gone to college, that I first told my parents what Koffey had said to me. "He told you that!" my mother exclaimed. "Why didn't you say something? If I had known I would've . . ."

"That's why I didn't tell you," I said.

I never considered following Koffey's advice. By now, I was getting pretty good at basketball and was starting to stand out among my peers. Bob Trotter even let me play on the RIC men's team. I wasn't going to let Koffey's kind of pessimism get in the way of my dreams. "There's college scouts in the stands," Bob told me, before some of our games. "You're good enough to get recruited." At those times, I told my teammates, "I need to go to school next year. Make sure y'all pass me the ball." Usually they complied, enabling me to put up a lot of points. It was at one of these games that I was spotted by Ron Lykins, the coach of the University of Wisconsin–Whitewater (UWW) wheelchair basketball team, who was scouting the Midwest tournaments. He introduced himself and talked to me about furthering my education and playing on the UWW team.

Ron became a regular at our tournaments, and he continued to talk to me about coming to UWW. He introduced me to Akil Muwatu, an African American student from the East Coast who was the leading scorer on the UWW team. Akil and I talked for hours and were both excited about the possibility of playing together. Ron also arranged for me to meet Monica, an attractive UWW senior who, coincidentally, lived in my neighborhood. When she came by the house to talk, all of my friends were impressed that they had sent such a "fine sister" to recruit me. After talking to Akil and Monica, I decided to enroll for the fall 1987 semester.

The small college town of Whitewater, Wisconsin, is located between Madison and Milwaukee, about two hours by car north of Chicago. Founded as a school for teachers in 1868, UWW evolved into a comprehensive four-year university by the 1960s. It now has a student population of over 10,000 and is the fourth largest of the twenty-six campuses in the University of Wisconsin system. John Truesdale, the founding director of the university's Disabled Student Services (now the Center for Students with Disabilities), served in that capacity for three decades, helping UWW become one of the national leaders for disability rights in higher education.[1] Truesdale also began Whitewater's wheelchair basketball program, which eventually became one of the premier programs in the country. Many of the best players and coaches have passed through this institution. From across the United States and Canada and from as far as Australia, Germany, Ireland, and Israel, they have come here to learn and develop their game.

In 1973, with some grant money from the Wisconsin Division of Vocational Rehabilitation, Truesdale bought fifteen sports model chairs, which, by today's standards, were still rather large and heavy. He also invested some of the grant money into remodeling the locker room, so that the players had accessible showers, toilet facilities, and gym lockers. The first year he attracted only five students to play, not enough to field a competitive team. But over time, he expanded the program, and as players graduated and went out into the work world, they started teams of their own that competed with each other in organized tournaments around the state.

Truesdale was also the team's coach. Although he knew something about coaching basketball, he knew nothing about the wheelchair game per se. In fact, coaching strategy for wheelchair basketball had yet to be developed.[2] For the first few years, the team floundered. But in 1981, when Truesdale stepped down as coach, he handed the new coach, Frank Burns, a squad of fifteen competitive players. In Burns's second year, he led the Rolling Warhawks, as the team became known, to its first intercollegiate championship. Burns coached the UWW team for five years, until he left to pursue a career in sports marketing. Ron Lykins was his successor. I never regretted following Ron's advice about coming to UWW.

The night before I left for Whitewater, I couldn't sleep. I felt as nervous as I had been when I came home from RIC. I really didn't know what to expect. The next day, my parents, Maurice, and I loaded up the car and headed north on I-94. We drove past the Great America amusement park and turned onto Highway 20. All of a sudden, we were in the country. I looked out at the cornfields and the cows. I'd seen cows on television, but never close up; they didn't have them at the zoo. "This is in the middle of nowhere," I thought. "What have I gotten myself into?"

When we arrived at UWW, Ron showed us around campus and got me set up in my dorm room. He introduced us to Truesdale and some other friendly people who made me feel welcome. Then my parents said they needed to leave before it got dark. I begged them to stay a little longer, but they seemed adamant about wanting to get "out of Dodge."

I was nervous about being in a virtually all-white environment. Almost everyone I'd previously known was black. The only white person I'd ever had extended contact with was Jerry Aiers. Jerry was a friend of Dobby's whom he'd met when he was attending school in Iowa for a while. When Dobby came back to Chicago, he brought Jerry with him. Jerry ended up living at our house for a few months because Dobby's mother wouldn't let Jerry stay with her. We got into a lot of fights with other gang members for hanging out with Jerry, especially when he wanted to identity himself as a Black P Stone. I told Jerry to say that he was White P Stone. Everyone who met Jerry was curious and asked him a lot of questions about white people, which often annoyed Jerry to no end.

My memory of how people reacted to Jerry made me apprehensive about how the white people in Whitewater would react to me. My friends even warned me about the Ku Klux Klansmen who they assumed would be living in such a rural, white community. My mother told me, "They're just like us, Boonie. Mr. Truesdale said if you need anything, just call him. You're gonna love it up here. Before you know it, you'll never want to come back to Chicago." "No," I insisted, "I want you to come get me next weekend."

After my parents and Maurice left, I pushed over to the ice-cream social that the university held for the incoming students. I looked around the room and felt like a grain of pepper dropped on a table full of salt. Then Raul Ortega, one of the players on the wheelchair basketball team, rolled up to me.

"You must be the new guy, huh." Raul said.

"Yeah," I replied.

"So, are you fast?" Raul asked.

"I'm kind of fast."

"I'm pretty fast myself."

An attractive female student came by and said hello to Raul. After she walked away, Raul started complaining: "The girls up here are so nice. They always say, 'Hi, Raul,' but they won't fuck me. They talk to me, but they don't want a guy in a wheelchair. I'm 21 years old and I'm still a virgin."

"Who is this guy?" I thought. "I just met him and already he's telling me his life story."

Prior to enrolling at Whitewater, I had considered myself a fairly good student. Unfortunately, all too many good students coming out of the Chicago public-school system remain unprepared for college. Chicago Vocational High School had been easy, and I'd always gotten good grades. But I hadn't really learned how to take notes in class or to study or manage my time well. I didn't like to read and would just try to memorize the material without really understanding what I was supposed to be learning. Now there was no one looking over my shoulder telling me to go to class or do my homework. There were times when I missed class for a couple of days, and when I finally showed up, I'd be unaware that the professor had scheduled an exam for that day. There was also the added strain of basketball practice everyday and the frequent traveling, which didn't leave much time for studying. Thus, during my freshman year, I was on academic probation and in danger of flunking out of school.

During that time, I returned to Chicago almost every weekend to hang out with my old friends. I even got involved in drug dealing in an indirect sort of way. My friends had gotten into heavier stuff, selling marijuana and crack cocaine and using the money to buy guns. Occasionally they asked me for money to finance their drug deals. I loaned them the money, and they paid me back a healthy rate of interest, $250 for a $100 loan.

I was living a schizophrenic life, going back and forth between two entirely different worlds. In Whitewater, I was Melvin, a respectful college student who played on the basketball team; in Chicago, I was Boonie, a gangster thug who'd become something of a legend in the community. Kids would say, "That's Boonie. He's the one I told you about, the one who got shot by Bobby Brooks."

My word carried a lot of weight on the street. If I told someone to go out and do something, they would do it. Often I'd drive around with my brothers and friends looking for Gangster Disciples to beat up. There were a couple times when I tried to run down a GD in my car. One of these incidents involved my friend, Reggie Boston, who lived in a GD neighborhood. We had tried to run over a GD who recognized Reggie. That night a bunch of GDs showed up at Reggie's house, locked his mother in a closet, and beat up Reggie and his younger brother.

Reggie called all his friends, and we started keeping a security watch at his house. "I didn't know Reggie had so many friends," his mother said. She also didn't know that his friends were packing guns. My brother, Maurice, was one of them. Before I got shot, I had tried to keep him away from the gangs. But now, all the younger kids were gang-banging. If they got pissed off at someone, they would go out and shoot them. Over the next few years, Maurice was constantly in trouble and in and out of jail.

During one of my weekend visits, I was hanging out at the home of a girl I'd been seeing named Felicia. Kim and Maurice had just left in my parent's car to drive Kim's girlfriend home. Felicia, coincidentally, was also dating the other Maurice, Bobby's accomplice in the shooting. I was sitting in an easy chair in the living room when, suddenly, Maurice walked in with a couple of his friends. He did a double take when he saw me.

"What's up, homey? Do I know you?" Maurice asked.

"Yeah, you know me," I replied angrily.

"Aw, shit. Man, I'm sorry," Maurice said. "I didn't know what was goin' down. Things happened so fast."

"Fuck it, man. I'm still alive."

Then Maurice walked over to me and tried to give me a sympathetic hug.

I pushed him away: "Get the fuck off me. I don't need this shit."

Maurice stepped back. "Have you heard from Bobby?" he asked.

"Why should I? He's not exactly one of my favorite people. I got nothin' to say to him. I didn't try to track *you* down, did I?" Actually, Bobby previously had called me when he was in prison to apologize for the shooting and tell me it was a case of mistaken identity. My mother had answered the phone and insisted that I talk to him. I wasn't too impressed with Bobby's apology, and I quickly got off the phone.

Shortly after Maurice left, I heard Kim banging on the door: "Come on, Boonie! We got to go! We're gonna get Maurice! We got him trapped in his car!"

Apparently, Kim and my brother had spotted Maurice when they'd left and had rounded up Reggie and another friend, Jerome Isom, to help them. When I pushed myself outside, I heard someone shout, "Pop the trunk! Pop the trunk!" I knew what was going down, and my first thought was to get out of there. I began pushing my wheelchair down the street, but Jerome, who was a pretty big guy, grabbed me before I could get too far. He pulled me out of my chair and threw me in the back seat of the car. Then he threw my chair into the car, leaving the seat cushion, which had fallen off, behind.

I sat there watching as my friends tried to kill one of the guys who was responsible for putting me in a wheelchair. It was surreal. Reggie pulled out a gun and walked up to Maurice, who was trapped in his car. Reggie said, "What's up motherfucker?" and fired several shots through the car window. Maurice slumped over after being hit in his side and leg. Then Reggie stepped back and fired at the gas tank, hoping to blow up the car, but he ran out of bullets before he caused any further damage. At the same time, my brother ran around to the other side of the car and tried to shoot Maurice some more, but his gun jammed before he could fire a shot.

My brother and friends jumped back in the car. As we drove off down the street, I shouted furiously, "Whose fuckin' idea was this?!"

"We had to get 'im! It was our best chance!" Kim retorted.

"I got 'im good! I got 'im good!" Reggie chimed in.

"This is really fucked up," I complained. "They can place me at the house. There's a lot of people who know I was there. We need to find out if he's dead."

Word on the street traveled fast. Maurice had survived, but the GDs were planning to retaliate. I realized I had barely dodged another bullet and that I needed to get out of Chicago right away. I told my mother, "I gotta get back to school. You need to take me right now."

"I thought you were staying another night," she said disappointedly.

"No, I can't. I have exams. I have to leave now."

A few weeks later, Opie called me at Whitewater to tell me that someone had seen Bobby go into a club. Opie asked what I wanted them to do, whether I wanted them to kill Bobby. By then, I'd had enough of the endless cycle of gang retribution and told him to forget about it. Bobby was eventually shot and killed, although I don't know who did it or whether it was related to what Bobby had done to me. There were a lot of gang members who wanted to kill Bobby. Bobby's friend, Maurice, was eventually shot and killed, too.

By the time summer rolled around, I realized that I had to get away from my former life or I'd likely end up dead. I was worried that John Koffey had been right about being disappointed if I went to college. Maybe I wasn't smart enough to make it in that environment. It was at this point that I made one of the best decisions of my life. Ron Lykins told me that if I wanted to stay eligible to play basketball, I needed to go to summer school to improve my grade point average. I enrolled in an independent-study course with Alan Einerson, a counselor in the university's Academic Support Services program. Einerson taught me various study strategies and time-management techniques. When I told him that I'd never read a book from cover to cover in my entire life, he took me over to the university library and asked me what I might like to read. I picked out *The Godfather* and after that another Mafia novel. For the first time in my life, I started to enjoy reading, and I began to see that it was a way for me to broaden my horizons, to learn about other ways of living in the world.

Jackie Wenkman, an assistant director of the university's Disabled Student Services, also arranged for me to get a summer job with Whan Industries in nearby Fort Atkinson, Wisconsin. The work was repetitive and boring—I put thumb locks into windows eight hours a day, nonstop. I stayed mentally focused on the job and kept it entertaining by turning it into a game. I imagined I was playing basketball. My team was down so many points in a game and I had to score enough in the next thirty seconds to win. Then I tried to attach as many locks as possible in that time period, giving myself a point for each one, to win the game. This made the day go by a lot faster and kept my productivity higher than the other workers'.

When I got my course syllabi the following semester, I tried to read ahead. I learned to ask questions in class when I didn't understand something, and I studied more on the road when I was traveling with the basketball team. As a result, I discovered a new way of thinking and of seeing the world. In my philosophy class, the professor asked us, "Does God exist? How do you know? How do you know that what you know is true?" In my criminology class, we discussed the issue of black-on-black crime, something I'd never really thought about before. My classmates were studying the subject, but I had been living it, perpetrating violence against people who looked like me and were going through the same struggle.

I liked thinking "outside the box." But if I tried to philosophize with my old friends when I went back to Chicago, they'd say: "Man, you soundin' white. Why you trippin', tryin' to use all them big words on us? You think you smart, just because you in college and shit." They didn't want to hear about black-on-black crime or anything else I was learning in my classes. They just wanted to keep living the life they were living. I knew that I had to move on. In Whitewater, there was basketball, not gangs, to think about, and I became increasingly determined to make the best of the opportunities that were in front of me.

7. **A Motley Crew**

When Ron Lykins recruited me to come to the University of Wisconsin–Whitewater, he was mild mannered and friendly. Once I arrived at UWW, however, I realized he could give Bobby Knight a run for his money. Ron was the type of coach who worked his players hard and berated us for our mistakes, but who ultimately won the respect of the better athletes on the team. If he didn't like something one of us was doing in practice, he yelled at us incessantly and made us do "sprints" up and down the court. If someone made a mistake in a game, he called a time-out and lit into the player: "You fuckin' idiot! Is your head stuck up your ass?!" Several players actually left the team because they couldn't put up with his antics, but Ron's "in your face" style actually worked well for me.

During my first two years at UWW, we had a lousy team, losing games by twenty or thirty points. Although I was inexperienced, I was the best player. Ron put me in a leadership role and expected me to carry the team offensively. During a game against the Rockford Chariots, I was having a bad shooting night and missed my first seven shots. Since I was struggling, I thought I'd better get my teammates more involved. I started passing them the ball, and we got back into the game. Then Ron called a time-out. He told me, "God damn it, Melvin! Did you come down here to play?! Why aren't you looking for your shot?! Shoot the fuckin' ball!" So I went back out and threw up about twenty shots, missing them all. Ron yelled, "Way to look for your shot, Melvin!" And we lost the game.

Then there was the time I got hit by a player in a game against Southern Illinois University (SIU). I was having one of the best games of my life as we were cruising to an easy victory when the player punched me on the side of my face. I was momentarily dazed but not hurt. My teammates and some friends from Chicago who were in the stands wanted to rush the floor and kick his ass. I didn't think he'd done it intentionally; I just thought he was going for the ball and committed a hard foul. I went to the line and hit two free throws.

The next time we played SIU, however, the same player stuck out his arm and clotheslined me across my neck, flipping me out of my chair and elbowing me as I fell to the ground. It was a cheap shot and Ron was irate. He stormed up to the SIU player: "This is bullshit! You *don't* fuckin' touch my player! I'll kick your . . ."

Immediately the SIU coach, who also played on the team, stood up from his chair, walked over to Ron, and shouted, "You can't talk to my player like that!" Then Ron grabbed the coach's neck and started choking him. Ron's face was red with rage, a huge vein popping out of his head. I thought he was going to kill the coach.

John Truesdale, who was officiating the game, grabbed Ron and body slammed him to the floor. John gave Ron two technical fouls and ejected him from the game. "Nobody fucks with my players!" Ron yelled as he left the court. The guys on our team were stunned by the incident, but we felt good that our coach was watching our backs and standing up for us. After that, we started calling him Rocky Lykins.

Whatever people thought of Ron, I am indebted to him for everything he taught me about the game of wheelchair basketball, from the basic fundamentals to the strategy of winning games. Most of what I've accomplished in this sport is due to the solid foundation that he gave me. He made us practice five or six days a week, sometimes twice a day, and he encouraged us to work out on our own during off days. We lifted weights, ran drills, practiced plays, and pushed our chairs endlessly up and down the court. He held us accountable, treated us like athletes, and didn't coddle us because we had disabilities. Although his coaching style didn't work for everyone, I thrived under his guidance. If I did something wrong, he got on my case: "Goddamn it, Melvin! You're better than that!" I knew he was right, and I'd just go back out and play better.

Ron has mellowed over the years, but I still like to tease him when we occasionally get together. "You were mean back then," I tell him, as I remind him of the things he used to do and say.

"Come on, I wasn't like that to *you,* was I?" he replied.

"Oh yeah, I'm still going through counseling for the shit you put me through."

Ron took pride in watching me develop my game, but he knew I couldn't carry the team on my own. He had to recruit better players. Fortunately, he discovered Canada, or rather, Canada discovered him. He received a phone call from Mike Frogley, an up-and-coming player on the Canadian national team and an aspiring basketball coach himself. Frog, as his friends call him, had seen a brochure about a summer basketball clinic Ron was offering at UWW. Frog called to inquire about the clinic.[1]

Frog's disability stemmed from a car accident he had in 1986 when he was twenty-two years old. He was driving his Fiat Spider convertible, speeding, to see how fast he could get from his home in Ottawa, Ontario, to his family's country cabin. Around a bend, he lost control of the car. He wasn't wearing his seatbelt, and as he fell partway out of the car, his body twisted around and the vehicle rolled over his back. Paralyzed from the chest down, Frog had a twelve-inch, pencil-like stainless steel rod surgically inserted on each side of his spine to enable him to sit erect in his wheelchair.

Frog is one of the most competitive people I've met during my career in wheelchair basketball. We are much alike in that respect, and we both hate to lose. Frog's parents taught him to strive for excellence and to work hard to accomplish his goals. His father always said that there were three things a person needed to be successful in life, and particular amounts of each: "a pinch of luck, a cupful of talent, and a bucketful of hard work." It was fortunate, his father added, that the one thing that we all have the greatest control over is the bucketful of hard work.

At an early age, Frog played basketball with older kids in his neighborhood who regularly beat him. He didn't become discouraged, however, but only determined to try harder to overcome his deficits. He analyzed the weaknesses in his game and worked on those skills. If his opponents were overplaying him to his right, because he dribbled to the basket with his right hand, he worked on his left-handed layup. If they were playing him to drive to the basket, he worked on his outside shot. His attitude was "Okay, you might beat me today, but I'm going to keep working, and one day I'm going to beat you."

In many respects, Frog responded to his accident as I'd responded to mine. As he's told me, "When I first learned that I wouldn't walk again, I took a deep breath, literally for a moment, and got myself together. Life is too short to feel sorry for yourself." He told the hospital rehab staff, "Okay, now tell me what I need to do to get better." If his physical therapist told him he should do 500 push-ups, he didn't do 300 or 400 or 490. He'd do 500 and then ask if it was all right to do more.

Like me, Frog was introduced to wheelchair basketball while he was going through rehab in the hospital. At first, he didn't like it. Previously he'd been the starting shooting guard on his high-school varsity team—a solid double-figure-a-game scorer. He couldn't quite get used to not being able to float through the air while he was finishing a layup. He still wanted to get back into basketball, however. So he called up his old high-school coach and asked him for an opportunity to help coach the team. The coach agreed, and this began Frog's love affair with coaching.

When Frog arrived at the high-school gym for his first practice, he thought about mentioning the obvious fact that here he was, a guy in a wheelchair, coaching a stand-up basketball team. He decided, however, that he wasn't even going to mention it. If someone wanted to ask him about it, he would answer any questions. Otherwise, this was just going to be about basketball, about getting the players to be as good as they could be.

When Frog called Ron about the basketball clinic, he realized that the dates conflicted with a previous commitment he'd made. "Is there another time I could come down?" Frog asked. "I still want to learn from you."

"There's not going to be a lot of guys around in the summer," Ron said. "What if I come up to you and run a clinic there?" Frog said he'd ask around to see whether he could work something out.

The Canadian clinic did, in fact, materialize, and the following year, in the fall of 1989, Frog joined us on the UWW team. Ron told him, "You're the first Canadian player we've ever recruited. We went through a lot of trouble to bring you here. Don't fuck it up, or nobody else from Canada will ever be recruited again." Later, when Ron started yelling at Frog during practice, I advised him to "let it go in one ear and out the other." But Frog didn't need any words of comfort or encouragement from me. He had a tremendous work ethic, which rubbed off on me. I thought to myself, "Damn, I need to take my game up a level. I can't have a Canadian being better than me."

Another first year player that season was Eric Barber. I had played with Eric on the RIC juniors' team. Eric told me that one of the reasons he decided to attend Whitewater was that he could see how much I had improved during the short time I'd been there.

Eric was born with scoliosis of the spine. When he was three, the doctors became worried that fluid buildup in his spinal column could cause his brain to hemorrhage and kill him. A surgical procedure could save his life, though it might cause paralysis. As a result of the surgery, Eric has been unable to walk and has relied on a wheelchair to get around.[2]

Like me, Eric was introduced to wheelchair basketball through Bob Trotter. At first, he wasn't particularly enamored with the game. At thirteen years old, Eric couldn't get the ball to reach the bottom of the rim. He couldn't imagine how he'd ever make a basket, and he turned to wheelchair softball and track and field instead. About a year later, Eric and his mother moved to a neighborhood with a park just down the street from their home. The park had an asphalt basketball court, and after his mother bought him a basketball for Christmas, he started hanging out at the court for seven to eight hours a day. Although he played pickup games with whoever came along, he soon realized that basketball was a sport he could practice and improve at on his own. Eric eventually became a terrific shooter, one of the best in the game.

Eric was competing regularly with the RIC juniors' team when he had one of the most thrilling experiences of his life, which made him the envy of all the guys on our team. There was a TV series at the time called *NBC Sports Fantasy*. People could write in and ask to live out their greatest sports fantasy. Eric's fantasy was to play Michael Jordan in a game of wheelchair basketball. The producers thought it was a great idea, and Jordan agreed to the match. Before the game, Eric had the opportunity to sit down and talk with Jordan for about forty-five minutes. Jordan told him he would show him no mercy; he was too competitive to allow anyone to beat him.

The first player to reach twenty points, at two points a basket, would win the match. To everyone but Eric's surprise, Eric jumped out to a 14–2 lead. It took a while for Jordan to get used to maneuvering the wheelchair. After Jordan would miss a shot, Eric got the ball and shot so quickly that Jordan didn't have a chance to react. It didn't take long, however, for Jordan to figure out how to manipulate the chair. Eric's lead began to evaporate. The score was now 14–10. But Eric didn't panic under pressure. He continued to make his shots and won the game 20–14. Eric is one of the few people in the world who can say that he beat Michael Jordan in a game of one-on-one basketball.

Among the other players on our 1989–1990 UWW team were Ronnie Pulliam, Chad Siebert, and, of course, Raul Ortega. Ronnie was an older player who had gone back to school in his thirties. I called him Pappy, but he could give me a run for my money. Often we raced each other up and down the court. At first, I beat Ronnie every time, but this only inspired him to work harder, and after a while, he was able to hold his own against me.

Chad was another matter entirely. He wasn't very athletic and liked the socializing aspect of basketball more than the game itself. During my freshman year at Whitewater, he became my first college friend. Chad fancied himself a lady's man, and when he got drunk—something he liked to do as much as possible—he'd hit on every female he could. Since I didn't like to drink, I often chaperoned Chad to keep him out of trouble.

Then there was Raul—a decent player, but never one to dedicate himself to the game. He was a space cadet, and we were often annoyed when he routinely rolled into practice late. Ron had a rule that for every minute someone was late, he had to do one extra court-length sprint at the end of practice. As part of the punishment, he also had to do an additional sprint per minute with *all* the rest of the players.

So if Raul was twenty minutes late, everyone had to do twenty extra sprints while Raul did forty.

During the sprint drills, Ron expected us to keep track of the number of sprints we'd completed, and he asked us to give him the count. If a player knew the correct number, no problem. But if he did not, the count returned to zero. Raul could never get the count right, so we tried to signal it to him, usually to no avail. There were times when Ron got so mad that he'd throw a folding chair across the gym floor. In retrospect, however, we all have to credit Raul for increasing our physical stamina.

Over time, Ron started to blame Raul even when he didn't deserve it. During a game with the University of Illinois (U of I), Urbana-Champaign, I grabbed a rebound after a missed U of I free throw. Three U of I players surrounded me and tried to take the ball away. I was momentarily disoriented and threw up a shot at the wrong basket. A U of I player grabbed the rebound and pushed toward our basket. For several possessions, the two teams went in the wrong direction until Ron finally called a time-out. He lit into Raul: "Get your head out of your fuckin' ass!" The rest of us just bowed our heads and tried desperately not to laugh.

P layer personalities are not the only mix on a wheelchair basketball team. There is also the level of functional ability stemming from the severity of a player's disability. From its inception in the late 1940s, the National Wheelchair Basketball Association (NWBA) intended to provide "opportunities for any individual with a physical disability of the lower extremities, regardless of cause, to play organized wheelchair basketball." Thus, any individual who had a permanent, medically diagnosed impairment that made it "impractical, if not impossible, to play regular basketball" was eligible to play.[3]

As popularity of the sport grew, this inclusive mandate created a problem of competitive fairness, as some teams used less disabled players to gain an advantage. Ambulatory postpolio players, for example, and amputees or those who are only missing a foot or some toes, have full use of their upper bodies and have an advantage over those spinal-cord injured players who have restricted upper-body movement. Thus, some players are able to lean out of their chairs to shoot or pass, grab a rebound, receive a pass, or pick up the ball from the floor. Others have little or no sitting balance without using leg straps or supporting themselves with the back of their chair, or they need to hold onto at least one arm of the chair in order to move their trunk frontally or laterally.

In the 1960s, the NWBA introduced a threefold player classification scheme that has undergone modification over time to remedy this problem. To understand this system, one needs to know a little about the structure of the spinal column. From top to bottom, the spine consists of five regions: the cervical (neck), thoracic (chest), lumbar (lower back), sacral (hip), and coccygeal (tailbone) regions. The cervical region consists of seven vertebrae, descending from C1 to C7, while the thoracic descends from T1 to T12, and the lumbar from L1 to L5. Below the lumbar region are five fused vertebrae of the sacral region and four fused vertebrae of the coccygeal region. In general, the higher the level of impairment, the greater the loss of movement function. In my case, the bullet entered my back at about the T10 level and moved down through my body, lodging in my tailbone. Fortunately, my spinal cord was not severed, and I am able to use my hip muscles.

Under the current NWBA classification system, *Class I* players, the most seriously disabled, include those who have loss of movement function due to an impairment occurring at the T7 vertebrae or above. *Class II* players include those who have movement loss due to an injury occurring at the T8 level and descending through the L2 level where motor power of hips and thighs may be maintained, as well as amputees with bilateral hip disarticulation (amputation through the hip joint capsule). *Class III* players include those who have other lower-extremity paralysis (partial or complete) occurring at or below the L3 level, as well as other impairments due to amputation (besides bilateral hip disarticulation), cerebral palsy, and other conditions unrelated to spinal-cord dysfunction.

According to NWBA rules, Class I, II, and III players are assigned one, two, and three points, respectively, and each team is required to put five players on the court who total no more than twelve points. Thus, a team could field a squad of three 3-point players, one 2-point player, and one 1-point player, for instance. Over the years, the classification system has increased participation of more seriously disabled athletes.

Player classification rules are similar for international competition, although here a more complex half-point classification scheme ranging from 1.0 to 4.5 points is used, with each team being allowed no more than fourteen points on the court at a time. The international system also uses a function-based evaluation, whereby trained evaluators observe a player's performance and movement capabilities before assigning a number. The international rules recognize that purely medical criteria are inadequate given the number of players, like me, who have incomplete spinal-cord injuries or whose impairment is near the upper limit or the lower limit of a particular classification category.[4]

In many respects, it's desirable for a player to receive as low a classification as possible, for one's playing time may increase if he uses a smaller proportion of his team's allowable points. The NWBA classified me as a Class II, and when I later played international ball, I received a 2.0. Some people think my international classification should be higher, but one of the ironies of a functional-based system is that a player can improve his ability through hard work, practice, and greater experience in the sport, which makes him appear less impaired than others with a similar medical condition. At the same time, when players are performing in front of evaluators, they will sometimes fake inability to do things that they can actually do. If a ball is thrown above their head or off to the side, for example, they won't even try to get it. Once a player receives his classification, it is difficult (though not impossible) to change it.

The 1989–1990 basketball season did not initially go well for what we hoped would be a more competitive Rolling Warhawks team. We continued to get beat by wide margins. Gradually we got better as we started to gel as a team, but we still lost most of our games. Nevertheless, 1989–1990 did have some notable highlights, among them the Spitfire Challenge tournament held in Toronto, Ontario. We were playing a Canadian community team called Red Deer. Everyone at the tournament expected us to get beaten badly, and Red Deer quickly got out to a twenty-point lead.

Ron called a time-out and started cursing us: "When is somebody going to make a fuckin' basket?!" We came out of the time-out hitting all our shots. I got into a zone. Every shot I took, from all parts of the court, went in. I hit four or five "buzzer beaters" just before the shot clock expired.

The gym was packed. Everyone was cheering. There were just seconds left in the game, and we were down by a point. Red Deer had the ball. They didn't need to score, just run out the clock. One of their players had been doing spin moves around me the entire game. He'd back his chair up to mine and hook his right wheel around my left wheel. Then he'd spin off and around me to get a clearer look at the basket. This time the Red Deer player made the same move without the ball, hoping to free himself to receive a pass from a teammate, but I managed to get into the passing lane and steal the ball. I pushed up the court and glanced up at the clock. Time was running out. Everything froze. As I crossed the half-court line, I threw up a shot. Swish— nothing but net! The crowd went wild! Ron jumped up and down as my teammates pounced on me in celebration.

Still, Ron knew that for our team to reach the next level we needed more size. Next year, with this in mind, he successfully recruited Grant

Strobach, one of Frog's teammates on the Canadian national team. Grant was a classic "big man," sitting high in his chair. He also was fast and a shooting presence from both the inside and outside. Because opposing teams had to attend to Grant, he opened up a lot of shots for the rest of us.

We dominated most of our competition that next season and were the number one seed in the collegiate national tournament held at Wright State University in Dayton, Ohio. Before hitting the road for Dayton, the players got together for a dinner and bonding ritual: drinking two bottles of Mexican tequila from which we extracted two worms. We cut up the worms and all shared in a ceremonial eating of the parts.

"Remember the worm, guys! Remember the worm!," Frog kept shouting as we won our semifinal game against Wright State and advanced to play the University of Texas at Arlington (UTA), for the national collegiate title. Before the UTA game, we painted our hair purple (the school colors) and shaved "Hawks" in each other's hair. I jokingly shaved "Haks" in Ronnie Pulliam's hair. The UTA players, in turn, painted their hair blue and shaved UTA in their scalps.

The two teams were evenly matched—we both had fast ball handlers, good shooters, and big men, but whereas we only had Grant, UTA had two big men. They double-teamed Grant, who got frustrated and made a lot of turnovers.

UTA also had Stevie Welch, a lightning fast player who later became known as the Allen Iverson of wheelchair basketball. I had played against Stevie in juniors' ball. When he was eight years old, he had been diagnosed with Legg-Calvé-Perthes, a degenerative hip-bone disease. Stevie was a scrawny kid when he was younger, but he had now added a lot of muscle.

"Stevie, you been doing steroids?" I teased.

"Melvin, are you okay? You're looking frail," Stevie retorted. "Is your scoliosis bothering you?" During the game, he shouted, "I feel like a bus driver. I'm driving your fuckin' ass to school."

Melvin in Warhawks uniform.
(Copyright 1994 by Paralyzed Veterans of America,
by permission of *Sports 'N Spokes*.)

I shot well that game, but it wasn't enough to carry us to victory. I was upset that Ron hadn't made any adjustments to respond to the UTA defensive press. With the double-teaming on Grant, I had more opportunities to break loose for a fast break or open shot, but Grant didn't get me the ball, and Ron didn't insist that he do it. Still, my play that season attracted a lot of national attention; I had led the Warhawks in scoring, rebounding, and assists. I received an invitation to try out for the U.S. national team that would play in the Paralympics in Barcelona, Spain, in 1992. It was an honor just to be invited. I'd been working really hard and had established myself as one of the best college players in the country. I thought I was a lock to make the team.

Sir Ludwig Guttman, a British neurosurgeon who worked with disabled World War II veterans at the National Spinal Injuries Centre at Stoke Mandeville, Great Britain, is credited with starting the Paralympics. Begun in 1948, the Stoke Mandeville Games evolved into an international movement, with the first Paralympic summer games held in Rome in 1960.[5] Currently, the Paralympics are held every four years in the same city as the able-bodied Olympics and include a variety of sports for people with disabilities.

The term Paralympics initially referred to the word *paraplegic* but later came to mean parallel, as the competitions were held parallel with the Olympics. Although the Paralympics is separated from the able-bodied Olympics, it bears little resemblance to the Special Olympics held for the cognitively disabled. The Paralympics are intended for elite athletes who train and compete with the same level of dedication and intensity as their able-bodied Olympic counterparts. Since 1975, international competition has also included the Wheelchair Basketball World Championship, or Gold Cup, which now takes place every four years in the off years between the Paralympics.[6]

Ever since I began playing wheelchair basketball and learning about the sport, it was my dream to be good enough to play at the national and international level, to play with and against the best players in the world. I was of course thrilled when Harry Vines, coach of the Arkansas Rolling Razorbacks and the 1992 Paralympic team, invited me to the tryout.

Things didn't work out as I expected, however. After the weeklong tryout that was held at U of I, I didn't make the cut. In fact, none of the rookies invited to the tryout were selected, including Stevie Welch. I thought that the selection process was rigged; the tryouts were just for show. I was devastated, depressed, and burned out. My rotator cuffs had been bothering me for weeks. At times, I couldn't lift my arms above my head without pain. My wrists and elbows were chronically sore, and I had carpal tunnel syndrome. Maybe it was time to walk away from the game I'd come to love so much, that I should just complete my college education and get on with my life.

Part III **Resolutions**

8. Fundamentally Sound

After my unsuccessful 1992 Paralympic tryout, I completed my college degree—I majored in social work and minored in criminal justice—and started working in the city of Madison, the state's capital, as a probation and parole agent. I was the first agent with a noticeable physical disability who had ever been hired by the Wisconsin Department of Corrections. The trip to Madison is a ninety-mile roundtrip commute from Whitewater, one that I still make to this very day. I prefer living in Whitewater, where I have access to the university gym and a community of other committed basketball players with whom I can practice and play on a regular basis.

In 1992, I still resented the fact that I hadn't made the U.S. national team, and the sour taste in my mouth wouldn't go away. Grant Strobach, my former University of Wisconsin–Whitewater teammate, talked to me repeatedly about coming back to the game, and, after a couple years sabbatical, I was finally persuaded to do so. I returned with a mission to make the national team that would compete for the Gold Cup in Edmonton, Alberta, in 1994.

Somewhere along the way I heard this quote from Jack Reid, a Diamond Director in the Amway Corporation, that's become kind of a motto for me: *"It's what you do when you don't have to do it that will determine what you can be when you can no longer help it. It's not doing what you like to do, but liking what you have to do, that makes a world of difference. And good things come to those who wait, but here's a rule that's slicker. It's what you do while you wait that gets you there much quicker."* I started thinking that I hadn't done everything I could to be successful in wheelchair basketball. I had the desire but not the dedication or discipline. I worked hard during the season, but I hadn't put the extra time in the gym to take my game to the next level. During the summer, I rarely played at all. Thus, my conditioning could have been better. So could my shooting and ball handling. I had yet to become a true student of the game.

At this point in my life, I also began reading a lot of motivational and self-help books to improve my mental concentration. At the elite level of any sport, there are so many physically talented players in the game. What often separates the winners from the losers is the mental toughness that they've acquired, the ability to maintain their focus under pressure when the outcome of the game is on the line. One book that I found particularly inspiring was about "TaoSports," the application of Eastern philosophy to improving one's mental approach to sports and to life more generally.[1] In that book, the authors view the physical game of sport as an "arena for the ongoing development of internal, psychological strengths." They teach that the athlete should have the "courage to risk failure, learn from setbacks, and forge ahead" and see "competitors as partners who facilitate improvement." The book, among other things, taught me various relaxation and visualization techniques that have enhanced my ability to first imagine and then enact positive outcomes on the court. These exercises became an important part of how I prepared myself mentally to play.

Since I still lived in Whitewater, I was able to train and play on campus with the other players. When I practiced, often after putting in a full day of work at my probation and parole job, I tried to shoot at least 300 made shots a day, 2,500 each day of the weekend. I also watched videotapes and began self-critiquing my performance, thinking, "What did I do well? What do I need to work on?" I thought more about how teams played against me and about the strengths and weaknesses of my opponents.

Looking back at the 1992 tryout, I realized that I hadn't done anything to stand out in the coach's mind. A coach wants to be able to say to himself: That player is rising above everybody else. He brings something special to this team. The U.S. coach for the 1994 Gold Cup was Brad Hedrick, one of the most respected and innovative coaches in the game.[2] I had played against Brad's University of Illinois collegiate team many times. I knew the system that he wanted to run and what he looked for in his athletes. He liked players who were quick, who hustled, and who were tenacious on defense.

I decided to transform my game to give Brad a reason to put me on his team. I would become a defensive specialist, the type of player who could "lock down" an opponent, who could take another player completely out of his game. I wanted to be the guy Brad called on when a leading scorer on the other team got hot and needed to be cooled off. I wouldn't be the go-to glory guy who scored all the points, but I would give Brad something no one else could provide.

My plan for drawing Brad's attention worked. At the spring 1994 tryout, I did everything right. I impressed Brad with my commitment to defense, with my mastery of the fundamentals of the game. To this day, I'm proud to say that Brad describes me as one of the most "fundamentally sound" players he's ever seen. It was an unbelievable feeling to know that I was among the twelve best wheelchair basketball players in the country, chosen to represent the United States in front of the whole world. At the time Brad announced my selection, however, I had to hold back my excitement out of respect to the other players who hadn't made the team. It's always an awkward moment at such times because the great joy that the chosen athletes experience is counterbalanced by the pain and bitterness that others may feel.

When I arrived at the U.S. Olympic Training Center in Colorado Springs to prepare for the summer 1994 Gold Cup, I looked up at the Olympic rings and felt a chill go down my spine. I thought about all the great athletes who had come before and had gone on to Olympic greatness. I felt that I was a part of something bigger than myself and that I was living out my dream.

I was in awe of my teammates. There was six-foot eight-inch Darryl "Tree" Waller, one of the biggest men who ever played wheelchair basketball. There was Reggie Colton. Trooper Johnson. All of them legends of the game. I idolized these guys, and now I was going to the world championship tournament with them!

Stevie Welch had made the team, too, and was my roommate at the hotel where we stayed when we traveled to Edmonton for the Gold Cup. Stevie was a quirky character who often riled his coaches who tolerated his antics because he was such an outstanding talent. (He was also a wheelchair tennis star.) On our first night together, we stayed up all night talking. When we finally went to bed, Stevie closed all the blinds in our room.

Brad had scheduled a mandatory team breakfast at 8:00 a.m. Brad had a rule: "If you're early, you're on time. If you're one minute late, you're late." About 9:00 a.m. I heard someone banging on the door.

"Shit, Stevie. We overslept," I cried, as I jumped up to open the door. "What?" groaned Stevie, still half asleep.

I opened the door and Brad stormed into the room. "Juette! Welch! When I say there's a mandatory team breakfast, I mean mandatory. That means it's not optional. That means you have to get your ass down there on time."

"I'm sorry," I said. "We had the shades closed and . . ."

"I don't want to hear any excuses. You hear that, Welch?"

"Yeah, coach. It won't happen again," Stevie replied groggily, as he rolled over and tried to go back to sleep.

"You guys are impossible," Brad gasped, as he marched out of the room.

In fact, Stevie and I weren't the only ones to miss the team breakfast, and Brad had to decide whether this was a battle he wanted to wage. Should he stick to his guns or let it slide?

There weren't any more mandatory breakfasts after that. But that didn't keep Stevie from arriving late to team meetings. At one meeting Brad barked, "Juette! Where's Welch?! Your *only* responsibility is to get him here on time." Before I could respond, Stevie came into the room. Brad gave him a stern look but said nothing more about it.

Brad was enamored with statistics—he had stats on every team that we played, every shot that they took, every spot that they took a shot from. He broke down the court into zones—they shot twenty-five percent from the left side, fifteen percent from the right side. Most of us thought it was statistical overkill. "We know everything about this team," chimed Stevie. "Holy cow, this guy had ham and eggs for breakfast!"

Brad had a definite offensive and defensive system that he liked to run on the court, but when Stevie was in the game, everything went out the window. "Stevie, when you're out on the court with the ball, what are you thinking?" Brad asked. "Well, to be honest," Stevie said, "I'm not sure what I'm thinking. I'm just coming down the court full throttle, waiting to see what the other team is going to do. I just react."

Brad paused for a moment before responding. "Well, I guess if he doesn't know what *he's* going to do, *they* don't either. You guys just get the hell out of his way and make sure you know what *you're* going to do."

At times, I could be as brash as Stevie. After all, I had learned the art of trash-talking on the streets of Chicago. After I made the team, I told my new teammates, "You know, when I was growing up, I was in awe of you guys. I wondered what it would be like to be on the U.S. team. Now that I'm here, I think you're a bunch of sorry asses. I can't believe I used to look up to you."

"Shut the fuck up, rookie," they responded, "get the fuck out of here," but it was all in good-natured fun. We called each other "gimps" and "cripples" and joked about how we became disabled. Political correctness we did not observe.[3] The guys teased me about getting shot: "What happened, Melvin? Did a drug deal go bad?"

"Yeah," I replied, "who's the dumb ass who got run over by a parked car?" This was a reference to Trooper Johnson, who would become one of my best friends. Trooper's disability stemmed from a drunk-driving accident in which he crashed his jeep into a tree. He got out of the vehicle relatively unscathed, but as he was trying to dislodge the jeep from the tree, the vehicle lurched forward and ran over his lower spine.

Trooper, whose real name is Lawrence, grew up as an "Army brat," traveling with his family from one military base to another. Many people consider him the best three-point shooter in the history of the wheelchair game. He's also the type of player who brings out the best in others, whether you're playing with him or against him. He plays so hard and relentlessly that you have to raise your game a notch to keep up with him.

Chuck Gill is another lifelong friend I met on that U.S. team. Chuck, who had contracted spinal meningitis when he was in his teens, is an extremely fast ballplayer and an offensive force from both the inside and outside. At that time, he also had a reputation as a player. He was once featured in *People* magazine as one of the sexist men in the nation. I like to tease Chuck about the "Sexy in the City" article. "Gee," as we call him, "you need to hook me up. How can I get sexy and get my picture in *People* magazine, too?"

Left to right: Chuck Gill, Trooper Johnson, and Melvin at the 2005 National Wheelchair Basketball Association tournament banquet.

At the Gold Cup tournament in Edmonton, the Canadian fans—who have fewer college and professional sports teams to attract their interest—treated us like celebrities, seeming to both love us and hate us. We were like the "Dream Team" of stand-up Olympic basketball, the favorite to win the gold medal. Young fans in Edmonton came up to us and asked for our autographs, then quipped, "Thanks. I hope you lose today."

I got a lot of playing time during the tournament, especially for a rookie. Although I wasn't in the starting lineup, I played more minutes than anyone else who came off the bench. For the most part, we had a pretty easy time of it, blowing most of our opponents away, averaging a twenty-nine-point victory margin in the five games that we played. In one game against Germany that was close in the first quarter, Brad put me in to guard their best offensive player, who was having his way against us. "Do *not* let him get up the court!" he told me. "I don't want him to be able to move." Brad kept me in the game the entire second quarter, and we went into the half with a sizable lead that we never relinquished. Later, in the final gold-medal game against Great Britain, my defensive pressure helped to hold off the Brits as we clung to a four-point lead with just a few minutes to play. We won the game by fourteen points.[4]

I was living my dream and making my mark as a defensive specialist. Then a funny thing happened at the closing ceremony. A mistake in the tournament brochure had listed me as the U.S. team captain. When my name was called to accept the gold-medal trophy for the United States, I didn't hesitate. I pushed my chair up to the podium and triumphantly accepted the prize. The trophy was huge; it must have weighed about twenty pounds. I grinned from ear to ear as I held it high before the cheering crowd. It was an unbelievable feeling being there, representing your country, knowing that you were the best in the world! When they played the U.S. national anthem, it brought tears of joy to my eyes. Although I had heard the words of the anthem many times before, this time they had more meaning. I felt a connection to them that I never felt before.

My success with the U.S. team was a breakthrough for the UWW wheelchair basketball program, which was emerging as one of the best college programs in the country, a place where you wanted to go if you were serious about developing your game. Grant Strobach and Mike Frogley, who played on the Canadian national team, contributed to this reputation as well. Eric Barber, too, was becoming recognized as an international-caliber player.

Before the 1993–1994 season, Ron Lykins resigned as coach in order to move to Atlanta, Georgia, where his wife got a job working on the upcoming 1996 Paralympics. Fred Wendt, who was earning a graduate degree in special education at the university, stepped in to fill the void.

Fred was able to recruit Joe Johnson (with Frog's help) and Troy "Wild Thing" Sachs, two versatile "big men" from Canada and Australia, respectively. Once Troy got to Whitewater, he brought in Jeff Glasbrenner, a local Wisconsin youth whom he'd met in the dorm, who became one of the best players in the world.[5]

Although I had graduated from college and was ineligible to play on the UWW collegiate team, Fred came up with the idea of forming a National Wheelchair Basketball Association community team that was sponsored by the university. In addition to its collegiate division, the NWBA organizes other competitive leagues composed of community-based teams not affiliated with schools. The Whitewater community team idea allowed students athletes to play with nonstudent athletes on the same team, enabling us to put together one of the best teams in the country, if not the world. Our practices were intense, and we pushed each other to get better and reach our maximum potential.

It was somewhat of an irregular arrangement. Noncollegiate players were ineligible for university funds, which were needed mainly to cover equipment and travel expenses. However, university officials felt that I (and Eric and others) had given (and were still giving) so much to the program that we deserved special consideration. We worked the summer sports and basketball camps that UWW offered for kids and helped with fundraising for the collegiate program. Our ongoing association with the university helped attract new recruits and keep Whitewater visible on the national scene. Everyone thought of us as role models—both as athletes and as citizens—for the other players. Thus, no one questioned the arrangement; it was "don't ask, don't tell." The university maintained its support of the community team until we received sponsorship from the National Basketball Association Milwaukee Bucks in 2001.

As it turned out, Fred was in over his head as the Whitewater coach. He had too many other commitments to concentrate on his coaching responsibilities. John Truesdale, the director of Disabled

Student Services, scrambled for a replacement. Frog, who had previous coaching experience even before coming to Whitewater, seemed like the obvious choice. Although Frog had used up his eligibility as a player, he was still on campus pursuing a graduate degree of his own in special education. Frog agreed to take the job on an interim basis, but he stayed on through the 1996–1997 season, after which he left to coach the men's and women's teams at U of I when Brad moved up to an administrative position.

Frog was a man with innovative ideas. He was instrumental in helping develop the youth summer camps and also initiated the idea of sending players into the community to do basketball demonstrations, make motivational speeches, and sell raffle tickets as a way to raise funds and increase the visibility of the program. As coach, Frog devised a number of drills to help players increase their stamina and speed and develop their ability to maneuver their chairs. He was always looking for new ways to give his team the extra edge. Troy and some of the other players had begun strapping themselves in their chairs to enhance their maneuvering capability. As Troy went up for a rebound, the force of his motion brought up his two front wheels, giving him greater height. At the apex of the tilt, Troy caught the ball and put it into the basket. A player who mastered the tilt—especially if he tilted laterally on one wheel—could achieve a height advantage over an opponent who was guarding him. Frog began incorporating the tilt into his practice routines, with some players being able to balance on one wheel for as long as thirty seconds.

The 1995–1996 collegiate championship tournament, which was held in St. Louis, was one of my most enjoyable experiences as a member of the Whitewater basketball community. Although I wasn't eligible to play, I was proud and elated as I watched UWW win a collegiate title, led by Troy Sachs, who scored twenty-seven of the Warhawks' sixty-four points in the final game.[6] Frog told Eric and me that the championship "was as much yours as ours."

The championship was memorable for another reason. I had borrowed my parents' conversion van to help drive some of the players to the tournament. The team also used a university-owned van that pulled a trailer with all the wheelchairs in it. On the way back home from St. Louis, we ran into an ice storm. The university van swerved, turned 360 degrees, and slid into a ditch. Fortunately, no one was hurt.

Quickly I pulled my van over to the side of the road. We called for a tow truck, which pulled the van out of the ditch. However, the rear end of the trailer was crushed and the players couldn't retrieve their chairs, which made for an interesting scene during a restaurant and restroom stop when Joe, Troy, and Jeff had to hoist players over their shoulders and carry them into the bathroom. (Joe, Troy, and Jeff didn't use wheelchairs when they were off the court; Joe had a Legg-Calvé-Perthes hip condition and Troy and Jeff were partial amputees who wore prostheses.) On top of all this, one of the players had an accident and wreaked a putrid odor. No one wanted to carry him, until Troy found a dolly to push him into the facility.

During this time, I continued to work as a probation and parole agent in Madison. It was an odd feeling at first, sitting on the other side of the fence, supervising people who lived in a world of crime that I had finally left behind. For the most part, I didn't reveal my background to my coworkers or my clients; generally, it just didn't come up. My past was my past, and I didn't feel obligated to disclose it to anyone. Occasionally, however, I might tell a client, "Yes, I know what you're going through. I've been there, too," as I explained a little about myself. But if the client asked, "Well, if you understand where I'm coming from, why don't you give me a break?," I'd have to tell him, "I can't do it. Me giving you a break doesn't help you take responsibility for your actions. You've got to get with the program."

When I first began working in Madison, which has a population of about 200,000, city officials were in denial about the emerging gang problem. "There are no gangs here," they said. "Just a bunch of kids getting into trouble." I could see that they weren't prepared for what was happening. One of the first cases that I worked on, a presentencing investigation on behalf of the court, involved a shootout in which one youth was killed. I discovered a lot of collateral information about the case from my Chicago friends. The people involved were affiliated with the Black P Stones and Gangster Disciples. They were among the youths from Chicago who were coming up to Madison to recruit new members and take advantage of the untapped drug market. Families were also moving north to escape, to find a better life for themselves in Wisconsin. Some people traveled back and forth, maintaining apartments in both cities. My supervisor didn't want me to put that information in my report because I'd have to testify about how I'd acquired it.

If Chicago didn't exist, there would still be poverty neighborhoods and gangs in Madison. You have the same problems throughout the whole country, but the larger cities do have an influence on the smaller ones. And as police crack down on drug dealers in one area, they simply move and set up shop elsewhere.[7]

I've become rather skeptical of those who dismiss or trivialize the troublemakers as "wannabes," as not "real" gang members. Even youths whom some consider "just playing" at being in a gang are still doing some of the same things as the so-called real members. Some of them are even more dangerous because they feel that they have something to prove. Their friends tell them, "You ain't shit. You're too scared to do this."

Oddly enough, some of my more unforgettable experiences as a probation and parole agent have had nothing to do with gangs but with mentally ill offenders. One was a young man who thought he was a vampire. He was on probation for biting a woman and trying to suck the blood out of her neck. He suffered from schizophrenia, and when he wasn't taking his medication, he'd hear voices that told him to do things. "I want to move to California," he said after watching *The Lost Boys*, a film about a group of vampires who lived in Santa Cruz, California. I had to bite my lip to keep from laughing.

"Why do you want to do that?" I asked.

"Well, there's a lot of people out there like me."

"What do you mean, like you? You got a job there?"

"No. I'll feel more comfortable out there."

As I gave the client a disapproving look, he replied, "Why you trippin'? You know what I am."

"No. What are you?"

"Man, you know I'm a vampire, right?"

"Unless you have a job out there, and a family, you can't go," I told him. "Have you been taking your medication regularly?"

Then there were the five women who when detained together in the Dane County jail, fought with each other over me, claiming "He's *my* agent." "No, he's *my* agent." Back and forth they'd go. One of these women kept trying to make collect phone calls from the jail to my office. Since the office didn't accept collect calls, the woman couldn't reach me. So she kept calling the operator, begging to be put through. One time the operator called and told me that my client was completely hysterical and wanted to know when I was coming to the jail to see her.

By the time I arrived at the jail, the woman had been placed in isolation. She had removed all her clothes and had spread menstrual blood all over her body and the walls of the cell. I spoke to her through a monitor: "You need to clean yourself off and get dressed, so I can come in and see you."

The woman tried to pull herself together but started crying frantically, fearing that I'd revoke her probation. She kept pleading, "Don't send me to prison! Don't send me to prison!" Later, at her revocation hearing, I asked the administrative-law judge to revoke her probation, but the judge felt sorry for her and didn't follow my recommendation.

Another of my clients used to repeatedly threaten suicide and was put on probation for harassing the Dane County Crisis Line. She discovered that she could get just as much attention by calling 911 and telling the police she was going to kill herself. When the police detained her in custody, I went to the jail to talk to her. I asked her what the problem was and she said, "They cut off my cable TV," even though she didn't have cable TV. I had to revoke her probation, not because of such antics, but because of fighting in jail with another of my clients.

This other client was a prostitute who had a $300-a-day crack-cocaine habit. Previously I'd gotten a call from the police department about her. "Your client is out on the streets again," an officer informed me. "You need to keep her off because the chief wants the streets cleaned up."

The woman was illiterate and had a hard time understanding the seriousness of her situation. "You can't keep using drugs and prostituting yourself if you want to stay out of jail," I tried to explain.

"Why can't I use drugs? I like it. It makes me feel good."

"You just can't keep doing this, being a prostitute either," I told her.

"Why can't I be a prostitute? How am I supposed to get money to buy drugs?"

I regretted that there were few community resources to help this woman and that I had no choice but to revoke her probation. I hated it when I had to detain someone in custody, and I didn't like how it felt when I had to put handcuffs on people.

I've never really felt comfortable with the power and authority over clients that I've had as an agent. I try to advocate for them when I can and help them through difficult times, but I'm also responsible for holding them accountable when they don't comply with the rules. I've also agonized over the disproportionate number of African Americans in the criminal justice system and the disparate sentences that are given to blacks and whites.[8] I've observed a number of times where judges sentence a young black male to the maximum sentence allowable under the law when I thought that a lesser sentence would have been more suitable.

One time I was sitting in court observing some cases with my supervisor, who was white. The judge called a defendant's name several times, but no one answered. Then he looked angrily at me and said, "Mr. Johnson, didn't you hear me call your name?" Before I could respond, my supervisor said, "This is Melvin Juette. He is a probation and parole agent." The judge apologized, but I could see in his eyes that he thought that every black male must be a criminal.

Another time I watched a judge who usually gave black males harsh sentences act compassionately toward one young black teen and give him a lighter sentence. I was sitting in the courtroom with a coworker, Dorothy Reynolds, who was also black. After the hearing, the judge came over to us and told us that he thought that the defendant had a lot of potential but had made a bad decision. He asked Dorothy whether she was the defendant's mother. When she said, "No. I'm a probation and parole agent," he was embarrassed for having made this assumption. From the look on his face, however, I thought he was going to go back and resentence the defendant and give him more time.

After several incidents like these, I've felt apprehensive at times about my chosen profession, even more so because many of my African American clients have distrusted me for working for "the man" and playing a role in keeping blacks down. All I can tell them is that "it took getting shot to change my life. Hopefully that won't have to happen to you before you turn your life around. You can make a better life for yourself, but you need to make better decisions and take advantage of the opportunities you have."

In addition to work and basketball, my personal life was taking a new direction, as I was spending more and more time with Sue, a UWW student I'd met at a party at Chad Siebert's apartment. A few of us were sitting around talking, drinking, and smoking a joint. Chad was talking to Sue, who asked him whether I was seeing anyone. Chad pulled me aside and said, "Dude, she is hot. You have to talk to her." Sue and I spent the rest of the evening talking and getting to know each other.

Sue was white, and when we began dating, we got mixed reactions from people, some of whom were obviously displeased with our interracial relationship. We hadn't anticipated that we were crossing a racial line that was considered taboo by some people. This attitude was prevalent among both whites and blacks. Some of Sue's African American women friends even stopped talking to her.[9] Sue and I didn't feel that we had to stop seeing each other just because other people had a problem with interracial relationships. Still we waited some time before Sue introduced me to her parents.

Sue's parents were rural Wisconsinites who had no previous experience with African Americans. I met Sue's mother first, who was supportive of our relationship and tried to ease things with her father. But he wasn't too keen on his daughter dating a black man in a wheelchair and didn't want to meet me. Besides his racial prejudice, he was worried that a man with a disability wouldn't be able to provide for a family. As Sue and I got more serious, we knew we were postponing the inevitable. The breakthrough came on Sue's birthday. Her parents wanted to take her out to dinner with some other members of her family. Sue told them she wouldn't go unless I could come along. Her parents were apprehensive but agreed.

At the restaurant, I ended up sitting next to Sue's father, Richard, who seemed uncomfortable if not downright hostile. Everyone was worried, and you could feel the tension in the air. They wondered what would happen if Richard said something rude or provocative to me. Richard broke the ice by asking me what I thought of the Persian

Gulf War. We found that we shared some of the same views about Iraq and about a lot of other subjects as well. To everyone's surprise, Richard invited me back to his house after dinner, and we spent the rest of the evening talking about life, politics, and sports. Richard was a man very much like my father, someone who worked hard to provide for his family and who wanted his children to be happy. Upon learning that I was a probation and parole agent, he disclosed that he had spent some time in prison (for burglary), something he never talked about with anyone.

After that evening, I was invited to all of Sue's family functions. Once the family had gotten to know me, my race and disability no longer mattered. Every year, however, the family alternated hosting Christmas with Richard's twin brother. This man was an outright racist who used derogatory racial epithets in his speech. He said flatly that I was not welcome in his home. Richard was so enraged that he told his brother that none of them would come without me. The man eventually reneged and over time, we became friends, too. Neither Richard nor his brother had any personal reason to dislike African Americans, for they had never interacted with people of color. Their prejudice derived not from their own experience but from stereotypical things they'd been told by others or seen in the media.

After dating for several years, Sue and I married in 1995. The marriage lasted a little over a year. Our divorce had nothing to do with race, however. Neither did it have anything to do with my disability, other than my commitment to basketball, which took its toll on our relationship, especially when I traveled.[10] Sue wanted more of my time, thought I was neglecting her and having too much fun without her, and didn't like having to take care of our household affairs alone when I was gone. When I wouldn't sacrifice by basketball career for her, we started arguing more and more. Over time, we became less interested in each other's lives and grew apart. Neither of us was happy in the marriage, and it soon came to an end.

9. **Lost and Found**

By the early 1990s, as I was coming onto the national wheel-chair basketball scene, the University of Wisconsin–Whitewater had achieved a national reputation of its own as one of the premier universities for students with disabilities, offering a range of services that were available at fewer than a half dozen other educational institutions in the country. The facilities on the campus were almost entirely accessible, with curb cuts, ramps, elevators, automatic doors, lowered drinking fountains, adapted lavatory facilities, and plenty of designated parking stalls. UWW offered a number of specialized services to students, including academic and career counseling, instructional aids, transportation assistance, liaison with government and community agencies, and recreational and sports opportunities. The sight of students in wheelchairs on campus was commonplace. It was a supportive and progressive environment for people with disabilities.

In the winter of 1993, Jackie Wenkman of UWW Disabled Student Services got a call from a friend in Oconto, a town of fewer than

5,000 people in northern Wisconsin. "There's a little boy up here," said the friend. "He's been in a car accident and he's just lost, rotting away. Is there anything you can do for him, get him involved in something constructive?"[1]

Wenkman gave Ron Lykins, still the wheelchair basketball coach at the time, a call. Ron bounced the idea around with Mike Frogley, who was then a graduate student in special education. "There must be other kids out there like this," they said to each other. "How about putting together a summer sports camp?" Ron assigned Frog the task of setting up the camp.

The little red-haired boy who precipitated the idea for the camp was Jeremy Lade. Prior to his accident, Jeremy played sports of all kinds, especially baseball, and was better than average for his age. The accident occurred on a summer trip he was taking with his family when he was eight years old. It was a foggy morning, and the truck that pulled in front of their car on a bypass didn't see the Lades' vehicle. Jeremy's seatbelt was resting too high, apparently due to a design defect. As the truck hit the car, Jeremy jolted forward, bending at his navel rather than his waist, shattering the vertebrae in his back.

Needless to say, it was a tough adjustment, especially for a youth his age. Jeremy had never even seen a person in a wheelchair, and it was a daily struggle to learn how to use it to get where he needed to go. The Lades' home wasn't accessible, and a ramp had to be installed and the front door widened to enable him to get into the house. He also had to switch elementary schools and make new friends because the school he'd been attending wasn't accessible. There were no curb cuts in Oconto, and Jeremy had to learn how to "jump" up and down curbs, a rather painful process that gave him many a bump on the back of his head.

By middle school, the adjustment got a little easier. Jeremy's new friends included him in the sports they played. When they played baseball (hardball), he hit from his chair; sometimes they used a designated runner and sometimes he pushed himself around the bases.

In the field, he pitched or played first base, positions that didn't require as much mobility. Jeremy was a competitor and wanted to prove to everyone that he was still an athlete even though he used a wheelchair.

When he was thirteen years old, Jeremy attended summer camp at Camp Wabeek, an Easter Seals program in the Wisconsin Dells. At Camp Wabeek, he was introduced to a variety of sports, including swimming, canoeing, archery, and basketball. Many kids at the camp had more severe impairments, and Jeremy found that he was more athletic—and more motivated to be athletic—than most. He needed a greater challenge and jumped at the opportunity to attend the first Whitewater wheelchair sports camp in the summer of 1993, which was attended by twenty youths.

At the UWW camp, Jeremy went swimming, learned karate, pushed track, and played tennis and touch football.[2] But basketball was his passion. He watched me and the other Whitewater players scrimmage and was as much in awe of us as I'd been of my U.S. teammates. We told him about the National Wheelchair Basketball Association and about the Paralympics and Gold Cup. "That exists? I could do that?" he asked in disbelief. We could all see that Jeremy had a lot of potential; he was the most athletic kid at the camp. "It'll take a lot of work," we told him. "But if you're willing to keep at it, you can do it."

After the initial success of the sports camp, Frog also developed a summer basketball program for kids, as well as a monthly weekend outreach program for those who wanted to play more competitively. As Jeremy participated in these activities, I took him under my wing. I taught him about basketball and gave him advice about living as a person with a disability.

I could see that Jeremy, whom Frog nicknamed Opie because of his red hair, had a natural talent for the game. He was fast, a good shooter, and a leader on the court. He also was an eager learner. If I told Opie to do something, gave him feedback about his play, he'd do it without question. I took a lot of pride in mentoring Opie and watching him develop into one of the top junior players in the country and eventually one of the top players in the entire world.

Meanwhile, the elation I'd felt after winning the 1994 Gold Cup was addictive. It was a feeling that I wanted to experience over and over again. I continued to train hard and was thrilled when Brad Hedrick selected me to play on my second national team. I was going to my first Paralympics, in my own country, down in Atlanta, Georgia! I'd be playing in front of a home crowd, with my parents, my brother Opie, and Sue there to cheer me on.[3] It was a dream come true!

Trooper Johnson warned me that the Paralympics would be much different than the Gold Cup. It was a much bigger event. Whereas the Gold Cup only involved basketball, the Paralympics included a larger number of sports. We arrived in Atlanta for the 1996 Paralympics a couple weeks after the conclusion of the regular Olympics. Some 3,500 athletes representing over 120 countries were there. We were led by Brad Hedrick and his assistant, Lew Shaver, two coaches who many view as the Dean Smith and Mike Krzyewski of wheelchair basketball, who assembled one of the best teams in the history of the game— Darryl "Tree" Waller, Reggie Colton, Randy Snow, Jimbo Miller, Tim Kazee, and my good friends Trooper and Chuck Gill. We had height, speed, outstanding shooters, and defense. Superior players at every position. People compared us to the Olympic Dream Team, which had just rolled over its competition to win a gold medal. We were the "Dream Team on Wheels" and were expected to win, too.[4]

The volunteers in Atlanta greeted us enthusiastically, an appreciation that we returned in kind. "You guys are so nice," one woman said. "I was here when the Dream Team came in, and they wouldn't give us the time of day. They wouldn't even say hello to us." One of the drivers told us, "Tomorrow's my day off. But I'm going to come in and take you on a tour because y'all so cool. I drove the Dream Team around, and the whole time they never said shit to me. They wouldn't even give me an autograph."

In other ways, however, as Paralympic athletes we felt a little like second-class citizens compared to our Olympic counterpoints. Most of the media and corporate sponsors for the Olympics had pulled out. The Olympic Village where we stayed was a mess. There was little quality food in the cafeteria, mostly sandwiches. The cable wires had been ripped out of the cybercenter. The concrete pathways and streets were torn up, making it difficult to push our wheelchairs around.

Still, we were excited to be there, and the fans were great. Words can't express the feeling I had as I anticipated the opening ceremony and entered the stadium with over sixty thousand spectators cheering us on. Vice President Al Gore officially opened the games with the theme, "Triumph of the Human Spirit." Actor Christopher Reeve emceed the event that included Teddy Pendergrass singing the national anthem and featured Aretha Franklin, Liza Minnelli, a sixty-piece orchestra, a nine-hundred-voice choir, a one-thousand-youth dance group, and the relighting of the Olympic caldron.[5]

After that inspiring opening, we focused on the task at hand: winning a gold medal. We could tell that we intimidated our opponents. At times, you could see fear in their eyes. They'd look at Reggie Colton and Tree Waller, two imposing black men, and think, "Holy cow! They're huge." Reggie was a double amputee who sat high in his chair. Tree, who had been born with some missing toes, had even played football in high school. Tree warned his opponents, if they tried to make a move to the basket, "Don't be comin' into the forest with the trees. If you do, you're gonna get swat."

The "pool play" format of the opening round consisted of a series of games played by each of a dozen teams that had previously qualified in the pre-Paralympic trials. The teams with the four best records would advance to the medal round. We emerged from the competition undefeated, the best among the top four teams.

In 1994, we had dominated our opponents, but this time, we didn't blow anyone away. I sensed that we weren't playing well as a team. When we'd get a rebound, everyone stopped and casually brought the ball up the court. We played passively, reacting to our opponents, letting them dictate the pace and style of play. But now we were playing Australia. In 1994, we had beaten them by thirty-six points. They had the same team as in 1994, and we had a better team. There was no way we could lose. The winner would play for the gold medal; the loser would play for the bronze.

Troy Sachs, my Whitewater teammate for two years, was Australia's best player. Troy hadn't been having a good tournament so far, and Brad wrote him off as an average player whom we didn't need to worry about. I warned Brad that Troy was capable of putting up fifty points and that if he got into a zone, he was virtually impossible to stop.

Troy got off to a slow start in the game, missing a couple of his first shots. That would've been the time to bear down on him. I knew from experience that Troy was an emotional player who was easily frustrated. If you got inside his head, started trash-talking him, he could get distracted. He also wasn't much of a team player. If he tried to do too much, he could get out of his game and hurt his team's overall play. But Brad didn't take my advice. Troy got on a roll, grabbing rebounds and making most of his shots. After hitting a three-pointer, he pounded his chest exuberantly.

Meanwhile, I sat on the bench, frustrated that Brad wouldn't give me more playing time. As we were behind in the game, he felt that we needed more offensive punch. Our offense went cold, however. We played tentatively and seemed stifled by Brad's regimented system of set plays, which didn't allow anyone to be creative. I sat helplessly as our team folded and made several costly mistakes at the end of the game. I was disappointed that I didn't have the opportunity to make a difference. As for Troy, he didn't score fifty points. But he did score twenty-eight, with twenty-two rebounds, leading his team to victory.

The blame for the loss to Australia can't be placed on the coach, however. We'd been overconfident, had felt invincible. We didn't match Australia's intensity. They simply wanted it more than we did. As one of my teammates remarked, "Every game against 'the mighty U.S.' was a gold-medal game for our competition, and we just didn't do it." Nor did we play good fundamental basketball. We threw up too many three-point shots and neglected the pick-and-roll. "We made 'Basketball 101' mistakes," Brad said, in the wake of the defeat.[6]

We were all devastated, stunned in disbelief. There wasn't a dry eye in the locker room. Trooper Johnson pounded his fist against the wall. "Stop it!" shouted Lew Shaver, "you're going to break your hand." "Fuck it," said Trooper, "I just don't care." I felt as if I was suffocating, as if somebody was choking me. I had worked so hard for this, pushed myself to the limit. I had wanted a gold medal so badly, perhaps too badly. Now all I wanted to do was get out of town, to leave Atlanta. None of the players wanted to play for the bronze medal. Playing for the bronze, someone said, was "like kissing your sister."[7]

Brad gave us the next day off to get over our disappointment. When we returned, we all talked about boycotting the bronze-medal game. But Jimbo Miller interrupted the negative mood: "Guys, if you think not winning a gold medal is bad, think about going back home and explaining why you didn't win *any* medals. Besides, you only win two medals in the Paralympics, the gold and the bronze. You never win a silver medal; you only lose the gold. So we still have the opportunity to go home winners." After Jimbo had his say, everyone knew he was right. We resolved to go out and beat Spain the next day.

Spain was no easy mark. They had actually beaten Australia in the earlier round. It was a tough contest, with the teams taking alternative leads throughout the game. We played in front of what was probably the largest crowd that ever had watched a wheelchair basketball game in the United States. Everyone was cheering wildly as we came out on top by a score of 66–60.[8]

Still, at the Paralympic medal ceremony that followed, I had a tough time listening to the Australian national anthem and watching the raising of the Australian flag. I looked at my teammates and saw stone cold stares on all their faces. Opie told my mother, "Look at Boonie, I think he wants to steal somebody's gold medal."

I left Atlanta feeling angry and depressed, and when I returned to Whitewater, I felt like I was beginning a downward spiral in my life. Not only was I disheartened about basketball, but the strain of the Paralympics was the last straw in my relationship with Sue. In fact, many of my U.S. teammates refer to 1996 as a jinxed year. Several of them also went through divorces, and one had a bout with cocaine addiction.[9]

In many respects, I wasn't very centered at that time. I hadn't really absorbed one of the central messages of TaoSports, which is to view success as only "one part of the process of sport," to understand that "performance is a roller coaster [that requires] the patience to ride the ups and downs" and to enjoy "sport for the [pure] pleasure that it gives."[10] Rather, I still had the same mentality as I had when I was involved in gangs; if somebody got the best of me, I wanted to retaliate. Now I wanted revenge against Australia. So I took refuge in basketball and dedicated myself to helping the U.S. get back on top. Victory would be sweet because the 1998 Gold Cup was going to be held in Sydney.

In the meantime, I accepted an opportunity to accompany the U.S. team on a month-long exhibition tour of Italy that fall. Less than half of the players from our Paralympic team made the trip, and additional athletes were added to fill the squad, among them Eric Barber, my Whitewater teammate. It was a great experience traveling abroad for the first time and visiting such famous sites as the Sistine Chapel and St. Peter's Basilica.

The U.S. coach on the Italy tour was Dan Byrnes, whom I'd played against when he was coaching the wheelchair team at Wright State

University. Dan liked to run an up-tempo style of play on both offense and defense. In a rematch against Spain, we blew them away by some thirty points. All told, we lost only one of about a dozen games during the entire Italy tour.

During the 1994 and 1996 tournaments in Edmonton and Atlanta, the team hadn't needed me for scoring. We had plenty of shooters, like Trooper, who could put the ball in the basket. I had concentrated on defense and on rebounding, setting picks for my teammates and getting the ball to the open man. I took my shot when I was open, but that wasn't my focus. With some players sitting out the Italy tour, however, Dan told me, "Melvin, I've seen you shoot in college. I know you can shoot the ball. I need you to look for your shot." Given the green light to shoot, I averaged about twenty points a game on the tour.

Following the success of our summer sports camps at UWW, Frog and I talked about forming a women's team. When I returned from the Italy tour, Frog asked me to coach the newly formed team during the 1996–1997 season. Since we didn't have enough women with disabilities who wanted to play, we opened the team to nondisabled women as well. This made our team ineligible for NWBA-sponsored events, but we were allowed to compete in Canadian tournaments because Canadian Wheelchair Basketball Association rules permit able-bodied players to participate. I enjoyed coaching the team and loved imparting my knowledge of the game to others. The women didn't pick up the game as quickly as the men, but they were willing to learn. Unfortunately, the team lasted only a couple of years due to a lack of interest among female students at Whitewater.

One of the able-bodied women who played on our team was Sheila Williams. Sheila was a physical education major with a recreation minor who also worked in the summer youth program. She liked playing wheelchair basketball and even scrimmaged with the men's team. The more time we spent together, the more we were attracted to each other. After my divorce from Sue, we started seeing each other regularly. In Sheila, I found the love of my life, and we married a few years later.[11]

Sheila's parents, Ron and Brenda, live in the small town of Prairie du Chien, which has a population of about 5,700. But unlike Sue's family, they had previous experiences with African Americans. Although Sheila and her parents were white, they had biracial cousins and adopted black children in their extended clan. The small-town/big-city divide between our families didn't seem to make much of a difference, perhaps because my parents were from a rural background

Sheila and Melvin at the 2005 National Wheelchair Basketball Association tournament banquet.

as well. The only cultural difference that I really noticed was over food. I remember one time my mother asked them, "Y'all don't eat pigs feet? Or ham hocks?"

"No. But we've tried frog legs," Ron and Brenda replied.

"We eat the whole hog," my mother said. "Every bit of it."

10. The Best of All Victories

The time for the U.S. team to avenge our poor showing in the 1996 Paralympics was finally at hand. But at the start of the 1998 Gold Cup in Sydney, Australia, we no longer intimidated our opponents. Our Dream Team mystique had been shattered, and the other countries were more confident that they could beat us. It was the first time that we'd gone into an international tournament as the underdog.

We surprised them all, however. Dan Byrnes was our coach, and he put together an unusually youthful and athletic group of players, relying on speed rather than height and skillfully rotating ten to twelve players to fuel a relentless full-court pressing defense and an aggressive offensive attack.[1] We marched through the preliminary round undefeated, easily defeating our competition. Then, as in 1996, we had to get through Troy Sachs and Australia to make it to the gold-medal game. It was the ultimate revenge match, something I'd been dreaming about for two years, only this time, Australia was the favorite to win.

The moment that I remember most about that game, the one that is frozen in time, involved a trip I took to the free-throw line. The Australian fans were going wild, waving their flags and flailing their arms as they tried to distract me, but I blocked everything out of my mind and made both of my shots. "Take that, Australia!" I thought.

We went on to beat Australia decisively by a score of 64–46. This time it was Troy who was devastated. When he came to congratulate me, he had tears in his eyes. I genuinely felt bad for him and told him I knew exactly what he was going through.

The victory over Australia wasn't enough, however. It didn't erase the bitterness of the Atlanta defeat, but it did entitle us to play in the gold-medal game. Our opponent was the Netherlands. We had beaten them in the preliminary round by sixteen points, but in the gold-medal game, the lead went back and forth. Paul Schulte and I alternated guarding Gert Jan van der Linden, the Netherlands' best player. When Paul got into foul trouble in the closing minutes of the game, the responsibility was all mine. I pressured van der Linden into committing an offensive foul, which fouled him out of the game. Then, with the Netherlands taking a one-point lead into the final minute of play, Trooper Johnson got hot and scored our last seven points as we came away with a narrow 61–59 victory.

We had won the gold, and I was proud to have played my part in bringing my team back from the disappointment of 1996. In its coverage of the Gold Cup, *Sports 'N Spokes* magazine described teammate Will Waller, another victim of Chicago gang violence, and me as "defensive wizards."[2] The team statistician told me I had logged more tournament minutes than any other player on the squad. More importantly, I was often on the court at the end of games, when the outcome was on the line.

The Gold Cup wasn't the Paralympics, however, and when I returned home from Australia, I felt a little letdown, a little unsatisfied. I had won two Gold Cup gold medals in my career, but I was missing a Paralympic gold. I'd have to wait until 2000, when we'd return to Sydney for the Paralympics.

The Sydney Paralympics that followed the regular 2000 Olympics was thrilling, far surpassing the 1996 Paralympics in pageantry. Over 4,000 athletes from 121 countries and 91,000 spectators attended the four-hour opening ceremony.[3] Unlike Atlanta, the food in the Olympic Village was great. We had physical and massage therapists available to us twenty-four hours a day. We had access to a drop-off laundry service, video arcade, computer center, movie theatre, and barbershop. Many of the volunteers joked that the Olympics was just a practice run to help prepare them for the Paralympics. We played our games in front of huge cheering crowds, as many as 18,000 to 20,000 people. We were finally getting the respect that we thought we deserved.

That year I became the energizer of our team, both on and off the court. I led my teammates in chants to get their juices flowing and stir up the crowd. To the tune of "Amen," we sang, *"Let everybody say U.S.A. U.S.A. U.S.A. U.S.A. U.S.A."* Then I went, *"A little louder now,"* and they sang the refrain again. Or we all got in a circle and chanted, *"Oo. Aw. U.S.A. Oo. Aw. U.S.A"* over and over again.

During the preliminary round, we defeated the home-team Aussies to knock them out of the medal competition. Then we faced Gert van der Linden and the Netherlands, whom we'd defeated in 1998. The winner of that game would play for the gold, the loser for the bronze.

The Netherlands got out to an early eighteen-point lead. I'd never been on a U.S. team that had fallen that far behind, but we fought hard to get back into the game. With less than a minute to play, van der Linden hit a shot to give the Netherlands a slim three-point lead. In 1998, Trooper's brilliant shooting had sealed the victory for us. This time, with the clock winding down, Trooper rolled up to the three-point line. A three-point basket would tie the game, putting it into overtime. Trooper put up his shot, which bounced off the rim. Jeff Glasbrenner grabbed the rebound and instinctively put it back into the basket as the horn sounded, giving the Netherlands a 63–62 victory.

My hope of winning a Paralympic gold medal was shattered once again. We were all disappointed and exhausted, but I didn't want to relive what had transpired in the locker room after our loss to Australia in 1996. I immediately went around to all the guys, giving them a hug and telling them they'd played a great game. "I'm proud of you guys. Keep your heads up," I said. "We still have one more game to play. Let's focus on winning the bronze medal."

Melvin reaching for a rebound with the U.S. team at the 2000 Paralympics.

(Copyright 2000 by Paralyzed Veterans of America, by permission of *Sports 'N Spokes*. Mark Cowan, photographer.)

Our opponent in the bronze-medal game was Great Britain. We'd beaten them in an overtime game during the preliminary round, as Trooper had gotten hot and scored all twelve of our overtime points. Great Britain was looking for revenge.

It was another close game, tied 54–54 as a Great Britain player missed an easy shot with seven seconds to go. Will grabbed the rebound for us and kicked the ball out to Eric Barber, who passed it to Paul Schulte, by now an emerging superstar.[4] As Paul crossed the center-court line, he threw up a shot from ten feet outside the three-point line. I held my breath as I watched the ball in flight. The horn went off while the ball was still in the air. Swish—nothing but net! The crowd went wild as all the U.S. players pushed onto the court in jubilation.

Winning the bronze medal in this fashion made everyone forget that we hadn't been playing for the gold. I realized that I'd been child-ish for the bitterness I'd felt over the 1996 games. This time I felt that the bronze was as good as the gold. I was finally realizing the TaoSport way; the outcome, the winning, was not as important as the journey along the way. I still wanted to win every game I played, but it had taken me all this time to shed my obsession with coming out on top.

Sheila had accompanied me to Sydney, and we stayed an extra week after the Paralympics before going home. After a day touring the city, we returned to our downtown hotel around 6:00 p.m. I surprised Sheila and told her we had tickets for the 8:00 p.m. performance at the Opera House and that we needed to get ready if we wanted to make it on time. "Are you serious?" she said exhaustedly, wanting to call it a night. "When did you get the tickets? What are we going to see?" I told her she'd have to wait and see.

When we arrived at the Opera House, I told Sheila that we needed to pick up the tickets at the will-call booth. As we walked around the building, the moon lit up the night. We stopped to look at the sky, and I told her to sit on my lap. I started talking to her about our relation-ship and how much I loved her. Sheila knew what I was going to do. I took out a ring and she started to cry, not caring that I really didn't have tickets to the opera. She said yes to my proposal of marriage and made me the happiest man in the world!

Following the 2000 games, the U.S. Olympic Committee invited the participating athletes—Olympians and Paralympians alike—to Washington, DC, to celebrate our accomplishments. They treated us like royalty, with a dinner at the Marriott followed by a gala reception filled with music and good cheer. They called it the Night of Cham-pions, and it felt surreal to be there with all these other incredible athletes. They showed taped highlights from both the Olympic and

Melvin with President Clinton at the White House in 2000.
(Courtesy of the United States Olympic Committee.)

Paralympic games. Everyone went wild when they saw Paul's shot that won the bronze-medal game. Goose bumps went down my spine. The next day we visited the White House and met President Bill Clinton and Hillary Clinton. The president congratulated and thanked each of us for representing our country. Who would've thought that a former gang banger would one day be invited to the White House to shake hands with the president of the United States?! It was an incredible experience, one of the most memorable highlights of my life, something beyond my wildest dreams.

Throughout the 1990s, our University of Wisconsin–Whitewater community team consistently fielded a nationally competitive squad, but we'd never won an NWBA championship. Although we had athletes who played for the U.S. and Canadian national teams— Eric, Jeff Glasbrenner, Joe Johnson, and me—other teams had players of this caliber, too. Tree Waller, Reggie Colton, and Stevie Welch, for

Melvin shooting at the 2001 United States Basketball Festival in Whitewater.

(Copyright 2001 Paralyzed Veterans of America, by permission of *Sports 'N Spokes.*)

example, played for the National Basketball Association (NBA)–affiliated Dallas Mavericks, and Trooper and Chuck Gill played for the NBA-affiliated Golden State Warriors.

The college-sponsored community team had always been an irregular arrangement, and I felt that we needed to separate ourselves from the university program. I thought that veterans' involvement with the college players was limiting their development because they were becoming too dependent on our leadership; the community team also took the university's focus away from pursuit of a collegiate championship. So I took the lead role in approaching the NBA Milwaukee Bucks about the possibility of sponsoring a wheelchair basketball team. After a couple years of negotiations, the Bucks' management finally agreed.

In 2001–2002, the first year I played in a Bucks uniform, I had one of the best seasons of my career. In the semifinals of the NWBA Division I championship tournament, we faced the University of Texas at Arlington (UTA), an outstanding college team led by Paul Schulte. Our relentless team defense and balanced offensive attack was too much for UTA, and we won a convincing 90–74 victory. Dave Durepos and I led the Bucks in scoring with twenty-one points apiece. *Sports 'N Spokes* complimented my play on both ends of the court,

Melvin dribbling with the Milwaukee Bucks' team at the 2002 National Wheelchair Basketball Association (NWBA) Division I championship tournament.

noting that I had scored "on a variety of shots . . . and on one occasion . . . [had weaved my] way swiftly through a maze of defenders to hit an eye-popping, twisting layup." The magazine also said that I had "shadowed Schulte all over the court, limiting the potentially explosive [player] to an unusually low [number of] points."[5]

In the championship game, we faced Trooper and the Golden State Warriors and came away with an impressive 85–67 victory. Again, I played a key role in the victory. *Sports 'N Spokes* wrote that "the entire Milwaukee team, and particularly defensive wizard Juette, applied intense defensive pressure, forcing Trooper Johnson to miss fourteen of . . . seventeen shots. Juette's outstanding defense prompted Golden State's excellent coach, Paul Jackson, to pronounce, 'Mel played the game of his life.'"[6]

Melvin holding the NWBA Division I
championship tournament trophy.

As I took stock of my basketball career, I had a lot to be me happy about. I had won an NWBA championship and two Gold Cup gold medals. I also felt rewarded that I'd been able to pass on my knowledge of the game to others. Jeremy Lade (Opie) had enrolled in UWW in the fall of 1999 and had become the starting point guard and leader of the collegiate team. I practiced with Opie regularly—and still do to this very day—and often we'd be the last ones remaining in the gym after everyone else had left, shooting basket after basket and egging each other on. When we scrimmaged with the other players, Opie liked to trash-talk: "I got the old guy. Geriatrics, I've been watching you for years. I know all your moves."

When I started to score, I'd retort, "You youngsters gettin' tired yet? You've been watching me, but were you comprehending what I was doing? This old man is running circles around you."

Still, it bothered me that I hadn't won a Paralympic gold; this was the missing piece of the NWBA–Gold Cup–Paralympic trifecta. I realized that the 2004 Paralympics in Athens, Greece, could possibly be the last opportunity for me to accomplish this feat. Trooper, Gee, and I talked about retiring from international competition after we won the Athens gold.

The first task at hand, however, was the 2002 Gold Cup in Kitakyushi City, Japan. But something unexpected happened on the way to Japan. I'd gone into the tryouts with a shoulder injury, and on the second day, I pulled my groin and strained my abdomen. I was in a lot of pain and could barely get in and out of my wheelchair. After I got hurt, I knew I wouldn't make the team. But I was shocked when Mo Phillips, coaching the U.S. team for the first time, didn't select Trooper either. Both of us were especially disappointed because we had wanted to step down of our own accord. Everyone else, including the players who made the cut, was stunned as well. Did Mo think that some of us veteran players were over the hill? On the bright side, however, Mo did select Opie to his first national team.

I took the experience of not making the team in stride and focused on all the positive things going on in my life. I liked my job; I was now working as the Community Service Coordinator of the Deferred Prosecution Unit of the Dane County District Attorney's Office. Sheila and I were going to Jamaica the next month to get married. I had secured the sponsorship of the Milwaukee Bucks and had won an NWBA championship, and served on the NWBA executive board and as chair of its Division I.

At the Gold Cup tournament in Japan, player discontent mounted. Mo had promised some of them more playing time, that they would be more of an integral part of the team. When he didn't keep his word, the players were upset; and when they tried to talk to him, he got defensive. The players also felt that Mo had no coaching strategy whatsoever; he just told them to go out and play hard. Previous U.S. coaches had had previous coaching experience and had coached players on college teams. Although Mo had been a phenomenal player, he lacked this coaching background. It seemed like he didn't know what to do.

Stevie Welch actually left the team, but the other players banded together. They felt they had enough talent to win, with or without a good coach. In the semifinal game against Canada, Paul led the team in scoring, though it took double overtime to win. In the gold-medal match, which was closely contested for most of the game, the

Left to right: Mike Frogley, Melvin, Jeremy Lade, and Eric Barber at the 2005 NWBA tournament banquet.

U.S. finally pulled away to a 74–61 victory against Great Britain. Eric and Will Waller, two of my Bucks teammates, received recognition as tournament all-stars, and *Sports 'N Spokes* complemented Opie's play, describing him as a "star-to-be."[7]

The following season I watched proudly as Opie and the UWW collegiate team emerged to national prominence. I attended all the games, cheering the team on and heckling the opposition. At the 2002–2003 national collegiate tournament, which was played in Whitewater, the Rolling Warhawks defeated Oklahoma State University to make it to the championship game. Their opponent was UTA. I held my breath as UTA nursed a three-point lead with just over two minutes to play. At the thirty-four-second mark, Whitewater tied the game, but UTA had the ball, hoping to take the last shot. Then Warhawks freshman Jeremy Campbell stole the ball and immediately called a time-out, stopping play with just 4.5 seconds left on the clock.

When play resumed, Opie received the inbound pass. Quickly he pushed his way to the top of the key, twenty feet from the basket.

Guarded by two UTA players who held their arms high, Opie threw up a shot. The buzzer went off as the ball soared through the air. It banked off the glass and through the hoop, giving Whitewater a thrilling two-point victory! We all mobbed Opie as pandemonium broke out in the gym.[8]

In September of 2004, wheelchair athletics around the world celebrated the twelfth Paralympic games amidst the grandeur of Athens, Greece, the site of the first Olympics. Some 50,000 spectators welcomed the nearly 4,000 athletes at the Opening Ceremony. International Paralympic Committee President Phil Craven spoke to the crowd, quoting Democritus, the ancient Greek philosopher, who said, "To win oneself is the first and best of all victories." Craven reminded the Paralympians that "recognizing and cultivating your unique abilities, mastering challenges, maintaining the balance between body and spirit—you set standards and give expression for many people, young and old, around the world."[9]

I had once dreamed of playing in the Athens Paralympics, but I wasn't there to hear Craven's speech. Mo was coaching the team again and several top players, including me, decided not to tryout for the team. Consequently, the U.S. came up empty-handed, falling to seventh place.[10] The gold-medal winner was Canada, led by Mike Frogley, who coached the team, and Joe Johnson, who contributed fifteen points and eleven rebounds in the final game against Australia. Some people blamed those of us who had sat out for the U.S.'s dismal showing, but as a result of our actions, the criteria for selecting the coach have been changed. Being a great player like Mo is no longer enough; the coach must now have more coaching experience and proven ability to lead an elite team.

Throughout all this, my spirit was unbroken. I had come a long way since my days on the streets of Chicago, since being shot in the back, acquiring my disability, not knowing what life had in store for me. There would be other basketball games to play, other challenges to meet. The words of Democritus make a lot of sense to me. Win or lose, I had achieved the best of all victories.

Postscript: November 2007

Sheila and I now live in a wheelchair-accessible home in White-water, which we purchased just after we married. Every summer my young nephew comes up from Chicago for an extended visit. I show him a life without the specter of gang violence. All the things I've learned from basketball—the work ethic, the challenges and joys of pursuing a goal, following your dreams, and savoring what is impor-tant in life—I try to teach him by example. I have gained so much from so many others; it is important to give back. Sheila and I have been foster parents to thirty-three children—from infants to teens, children of varying racial backgrounds. For the time that they are with us, we are able to provide a stable, loving environment for those who are in need. We are currently in the process of adopting two sis-ters, Melanie and Monica.

After a few years' hiatus from international ball, I tried out and made the U.S. team that won a silver medal at the Gold Cup held in Amsterdam in the summer of 2006. I was thrilled to once again be on the team. There is no greater honor than representing your coun-try in front of the entire world. We were a mix of veteran and young, up-and-coming players. Some of them weren't even born when I first started playing wheelchair ball. Half of the twelve players on the team were former or current students of the University of Wiscon-sin–Whitewater, Eric and Opie among them. It says a lot about our program that we had such a strong representation on the team. I am proud to have done my part to help forge a path that others have fol-lowed and to have continued to be a mentor for the new generation of athletes.

In basketball, we say that winning sometimes comes down to who wants it more and that success is defined by how far you bounce back up after you fall. I would not change anything about my life. Everything that's happened I had to experience to get me to where and who I am today. This is my story. Take from it what you will. If you are disabled, know that there is a world beyond pity, beyond dependency and charity. Don't let anyone else stop you from discovering who you are and want to be. Follow what Randy Snow calls "The Challenger Pathway": "It's our life *challenges* that reveal our *strengths*. From our revealed *strengths* we identify our *options*. From here we develop a *vision,* and in the pursuance of our *vision,* as Aristotle said, we 'realize our essence.'"[11]

Conclusion

Ronald J. Berger

A s I reflect on Melvin's autobiography, which has been a privilege to help him tell, it seems a remarkable life to me. When I think of the young man who sat in my classroom back in 1990, I could not have imagined the person he was and would become. What are we to make of his life from a sociological point of view? To answer this question, I return to the agency-structure theme that I introduced earlier in the book.

A Sociological Summary

Sociologists who study social inequality, who document and analyze the tragedy of social oppression, have reason to be cautious about privileging personal agency over social structure in their analyses. They have reason to be concerned that an emphasis on agency—on individuals' capacity to appraise their options, project themselves into the future, mobilize personal and social resources, and engage in adaptive, problem-solving actions—will reinforce societal neglect of people in need and of the discriminatory barriers that block personal achievement. They have reason to be concerned that believers in the myth of the "self-made man" will end up blaming people for their own problems, which could be remedied if only they tried hard enough.[1] Hence, we have the complaint about the supercrip in social analyses of disability, a complaint about those who seem to defy the odds and accomplish the impossible.[2]

I think Melvin's friend Eric Barber said it well when he told us, "Nobody is a self-made man. I am nothing more than the byproduct of the people in my life. They have made me who I am." The place to start when considering such influences is, in most cases, the family. In their study of disability rights and its effects on people with disabilities, David Engel and Frank Munger note that positive family relationships were typically more important than rights in the life outcomes of the people whom they interviewed.[3] More generally, Viktor Gecas observes that family context is probably the most important factor in an individual's development of self-efficacy, that is, people's belief in their ability to act on rather than merely react to their environment.[4]

In Melvin's life, as in the life of so many others, family ties were, on balance, a source of sustenance and stability. Cleo and Shirley Juette's child-rearing methods may not have been "state of the art," but they gave their son a foundation of love and economic security that served him well. They were, in Elijah Anderson's terms, proponents of "decent" values,[5] and they instilled in Melvin an appreciation of family obligations, the community of church, the commitment to education, however much he may have deviated from the path that his parents set in motion for him. Thus, Melvin was always a restraining influence on his peer group when others lobbied for and engaged in more radical actions.

Regrettably, Melvin's parents could not shield him from the racial patterns of residential segregation that exposed him to the ecological nexus of poverty, crime, and violence, where "might makes right" and the strong dominate the weak. At the same time, the sense of self-efficacy and masculine competence that he acquired through his accomplishments in this milieu helped him adapt to his later disablement, regardless of whether these accomplishments were ultimately the cause of his disablement. The survival strategies that he had learned on the streets could be transposed to the basketball court and to the challenges that he faced living with a disability. Melvin could still be tough, competitive, and athletic, someone who was in control of his own body, in control of his own fate.[6]

It is important to note that never in my discussions with Melvin did he ever frame his experience in terms of disability rights or tell me about an incident in which he had formally invoked them. Engel and Munger found this to be true for many of those they interviewed in their study. Engel and Munger also note, however, that, even in such cases, the disability rights movement has still had a "broad and persuasive impact on our culture" that has made possible an affirmative experience of disability.[7] Thus, Melvin's adaptation to his disablement must be understood in this context, as his successful life outcome was made possible by the people who came before, who said they did not want to be pitied or settle for being the objects of charitable goodwill.[8] Additionally, there were the pioneering efforts of disabled World War II veterans and innovators in recreational rehabilitation, like Tim Nugent of the University of Illinois, who founded the National Wheelchair Basketball Association and developed a game that has enriched the lives of so many who followed.

More specifically, in Melvin's case, there were the individuals and institutional resources *in his life* that translated this larger social movement into concrete opportunities for personal growth. At the Rehabilitation Institute of Chicago, for example, he received first-rate physical therapy and acquired practical skills that helped him live as a person with a disability. At RIC, he also had the good fortune of meeting Bob Trotter, who introduced him to wheelchair basketball. At the University of Wisconsin–Whitewater, Melvin had the opportunity to obtain a college education in a progressive environment for students with disabilities. For this, he has John Truesdale to thank for his role in developing the university's Disabled Student Services and establishing the wheelchair basketball program. Of course, there is Ron Lykins, who recruited Melvin to UWW and whose coaching helped him become a world-class wheelchair athlete. There are other university personnel as well, like Alan Einerson and Jackie Wenkman, who helped him get through his difficult first year of college. Then there are the other athletes Melvin met, who became his lifelong friends and mutually respected competitors and who encouraged each other to excel at the game they came to love. And there is the giving back of what he had received, as in the mentoring of Jeremy Lade, who has his own story of accomplishment to tell and who has already in his young life been an inspiration to other youths with disabilities.

Melvin often says that the shooting in the neighborhood arcade that caused his spinal-cord injury was both the worst and best thing that happened to him, that otherwise he might have ended up in prison or been killed. But we can only speculate about what his life would have been. He was majoring in cabinetmaking at Chicago Vocational High School and was planning to join the army reserves. Graduation from high school may have been accompanied by a gradual desistance from crime that has been noted in studies of youthful offenders.[9] It might not have taken a bullet in his spine to steer him on the right track.

But Melvin's real life is not speculation. It is a corporeal existence, embodied in his skin, in his muscles and bones, in the legs that don't walk, in the wheelchair that is an extension of his being and that gives him smooth access to the world. It is a body, to follow Arthur Frank's analysis in *The Wounded Storyteller*, that also has something to teach. It is a communicative body, one that reframes what is lacking—the ability to walk—as something filled with potential, which seeks a new way to integrate body and self.[10]

Just as Melvin's life was enabled by others, the telling of his story was enabled by a culturally available motif, what Frank describes as the quest narrative, a story about rising to the occasion to realize a dream or imagined possibility.[11] Early in his basketball career, Melvin dreamed of being one of the best players in the game and making the U.S. national team. Later he dreamed of winning gold medals in international competitions, a goal that he has only partially met to his satisfaction. Yet, like other protagonists in quest narratives, Melvin discovered that these external goals were not really the true objects of his desire. He found something more enduring, as he learned to treasure the journey along the way and found contentment with the life he has made for himself.

At the same time, the quest narrative, like the agency theme in social analysis, risks romanticizing disability or illness, for it can present the struggle of overcoming adversity "as too clean and the transformation as too complete," implicitly deprecating "those who fail to rise out of the ashes" of despair.[12] This latter meaning is one that we resist; we seek another interpretation.

Daniel Taylor suggests that stories of human adversity allow listeners and readers to "take comfort that even the worst life has to offer can be given shape, can be expressed—enacted—and therefore contemplated and reconciled."[13] A disability or illness that "sets the body apart from others becomes, in the story, the common bond . . . that joins bodies in their shared vulnerability."[14] People all too often assume that the social differences among us—whether they are differences of race, nationality, gender, sexual orientation, physical ability, or whatever—must inevitably divide us, constitute an immovable barrier between different groups. Too often society criminalizes, stigmatizes, or otherwise devalues these differences, denying us the opportunity to use our difference to "make a difference" in the world.[15] Telling the story of a life is one way to make a difference by making a connection to others.

Importantly, however, many people with disabilities do not substantially define themselves in terms of this or any other social category of difference.[16] Social identities may be symbolic constructs that people use to make sense of others,[17] but they are not necessarily how people view themselves. Engel and Munger found that the people in their study who were best able to narrate a "forward-looking" account of their life story were those who differentiated "their disability from their sense of self. For these individuals, disability was not the all-pervasive fact of their identity but merely an objective feature of their life experience that had its place among many other features."[18] As I noted earlier, Melvin does not frame his experience in terms of disability rights, nor does he frame his life in terms of race. When this issue came up in our discussions, he told me that he is "proud of my race and family background. I am the person I am today because of it." But he went on to say that being "a black man with a disability" is only a physical description of his appearance; it "does not define" him. Rather, Melvin views himself as a husband, son, brother, father, foster parent, uncle, friend, medal-winning athlete, "all these things and more. . . . It's unfortunate that some people go through life without getting beyond their socially imposed statuses and identities." Belying Kenneth Gergen's assertion that the contemporary self, overwhelmed by rapid change and multiple commitments, is fragmented and incoherent,[19] Melvin observes that "all these identities intertwine seamlessly to make up the person that I am."

Social psychologists have long noted that a person's conception of self is a social construction that is acquired through interaction and ongoing negotiation with others. But they have debated the question of whether there is an immutable or authentic "personal self" that shapes the "key organizing idea . . . around which we express identity."[20] To some extent, Melvin seems to support Louis Zurcher's contention that the self in contemporary society is not fixed but mutable in that it is open to a variety of experiences and adaptable to change.[21]

Melvin also seems to support to John Hewitt's observation that personal identity is no longer tied to ascribed communities (based on race or family background, for example) but is a product of choice or self-selection that allow people to shift "allegiances and involvements from one community to another, identifying with a number of communities over the course" of a lifetime.[22] At the same time, Hewitt also thinks that most people retain an immutable core or authentic self that defines the nature of their being. If there is one thing that Melvin believes lies at the core of his personal identity, it is, as he says, "I'm a self-confident, goal-oriented person trying to reach the goals I set for myself and my family." Melvin is, in other words, an agentive or self-efficacious individual.

Kierkegaard wrote that "to tell one's life is to assume responsibility for that life."[23] To tell one's life is also to assume responsibility as "a witness to the conditions that rob others" of their lives.[24] Melvin's story is not our readers' story. They define their own dreams, their own narrative thread that ties the pieces of their lives together. But Melvin's story is not that extraordinary, not that unusual. Everyone has had life challenges they've had (and will have) to face. What makes Melvin an impressive individual is not that he is some sort of supercrip but that he set a goal for himself and was willing to work hard and sacrifice to achieve it.[25] After watching highly skilled athletes who were at that top of their game perform and reading about the sport's legends in *Sports 'N Spokes* magazine, pursuing this level of accomplishment became Melvin's passion. These men modeled what a wheelchair athlete was and could become. Along the way in pursuit of his goal, Melvin adopted a philosophy of life from Tao-Sports[26] and other self-help, motivational books like Randy Snow's *Pushing Forward*.[27] Even an Amway aphorism was inspiration to him: "Good things come to those who wait, but here's a rule that's slicker. It's what you do while you wait that gets you there much quicker" (see Chapter 8).

Frank doubts that is possible in this day and age for people to embark on a truly original or authentic path in response to an illness or disability. The public domain is replete with the self-help and recovery narratives of the likes that fortified Melvin, rhetorics of self-change[28] or enabling technologies of the self[29] that model a way through one's predicament. The quest narrative itself is a generalized archetype that serves a similar function. These narratives are "opened-ended resources" that challenge the wounded to think of their lives in positive and hopeful terms while also preparing them for the hard work that lies ahead.[30] This work is not entirely or even primarily physical, however, for it entails the work of reconstructing identity, opposing discrediting views of disability in favor of crediting ones.[31] To be sure, competitive wheelchair sports are not for everyone who is disabled. Many may wish to play only casually and many not at all. But for those who are so inclined, wheelchair sports is a way to challenge stigmatizing characterizations of people with disabilities and embrace rather than reject their impairments.

Frank notes that personal growth in the face of an epiphanic moment or life event is a socially constructed experience.[32] To experience the onset of disability as an opportunity for growth requires a social milieu in which such experiences are viewed as possible or even expected. We are indeed fortunate, I think, to live in such an era, and it is my belief that it will continue to get better. Although I am a realist enough to understand the challenges for people with disabilities that lie ahead, I am not a cynical postmodernist who thinks that social progress is an illusion.[33] I often find myself coming back to a favorite quote from A. Manette Ansay, who suffered an illness that put her in a wheelchair for an extended period of her life. In her memoir, Ansay writes, "It's not that I believe the things that happen to us happen for a reason ... [or] that things have a way of working out for the best. . . . But I do believe that each of us has the ability to decide how we'll react to the random circumstances of our lives, and that our reaction can shape future circumstances, affect opportunities, [and] open new doors."[34]

A Tribute to Basketball

That I have found wheelchair basketball an area through which I have pursued my familial engagement with disability (i.e., my daughter's disability) is perhaps not surprising.[35] I grew up in Los Angeles, with Chamberlain, Baylor, and West. Then came Kareem and Magic, followed by Kobe and Shaq. Enjoying their athletic feats has been one of my guilty pleasures; among academics, spectator sport is not high art. Of course, these men did not play the game while sitting in a chair. They could reach the rim of the hoop by catapulting themselves through the air or simply standing tall. But the love of the game knows no boundaries between the able-bodied and the disabled.

In 1891, James Naismith, a physical education teacher at a YMCA Training School in Springfield, Massachusetts, invented the game of basketball so that youths could have a competitive sport to play indoors during the winter months.[36] According to John Edgar Wideman's account, Naismith envisioned the sport as a means of promoting healthy bodies for spiritually healthy Christians and arguably couldn't have anticipated how popular the game would become among players and fans alike.[37] He certainly couldn't have anticipated the game's cultural impact on African Americans. (Professional teams were segregated for decades, and it was 1950 before the first black player was signed by what was previously an all-white team.) Neither could Naismith have anticipated that the game he created would be played and enjoyed by people in wheelchairs.

Basketball aficionados have meditated about the reasons so many people have been taken with the game. Dennis Trudell thinks it has something to do with the way the game frames space and time. For one thing, it simply requires less space than a football or baseball field, which partly explains "why it is played in inner cities where ballfields are an extravagance we're apparently not willing to provide. . . . And within that confined area, the yearning is always for empty space: the yard to a defender's left, the bit of it above his or her palm, the sacred circle of it waiting above grunts and sneaker squeaks. We maneuver for inches out there; we fill that bright orange (or rusted outdoor) hoop through amazingly precise calibrations of hand and arm and air and ball."[38]

Wideman, commenting on the playground game revered by inner-city African Americans, thinks of the basketball court as a place where people go to fill a void in their lives, a missing father perhaps, or where they seek "refuge from a hostile world." It is a place where they can be someone else, "act out a symbolic version of who they are [or] who they want to be," even imagine a different life for themselves. All this, however, requires learning "what it costs to play," putting in the hard work, the hours of practice and dedication that it takes to make yourself a better player, refusing to "settle into a comfort zone" or to "accept limits" on how good you can be.[39] Thus, you can perhaps see how a game with this appeal would attract someone like Melvin who was struggling to find his way out of the state of liminality that marked the initial stage of his recovery from his gunshot injury.

The attraction of basketball also has something to do with the time dimension of the game, which for the fan, Trudell says, fits more comfortably into an afternoon or evening, unlike a seemingly endless baseball or football game. There is a time constraint that keeps the game moving, so much time to get the ball across the half-court line, so much time to put up a shot. And there is the drama that can transpire with just a few seconds to play, with game-winning shots that go in as the clock runs out.[40]

More importantly, for the players, the time dimension demands that you live in the moment, for to play "the game well requires all your attention," demands that you be "acutely alert to what you're experiencing," be "the experience," and forget about your multiple selves (past, present, and future) and all the obligations these entail.[41] I think of Melvin when Wideman writes that, for him, nothing besides basketball offered "the clarifying, cleansing unity" of the self. For Wideman, like Melvin, basketball always stood "above the fray, . . . the countless hours committed to it unregretted," the one thing that remained "untouchable over the years as I developed and revised blueprints for making the most profitable use of my time."[42]

To those who don't "get it" about basketball, it may seem rather odd that a game—"a game that starts out as messing around, trying to accomplish something vaguely challenging and fun, throw a ball through a hoop, a fun, silly kind of trick at first till you decide you want to do it better"—could carry so much meaning for some people.[43] To me, it seems wonderful, however, that something as simple as a game could be so replete with possibility, that it could be a disabled man's salvation, a way for him and others like him to transform, even transcend, disability. I think James Naismith would have been pleased.

Notes

Introduction

1. Doris Zames Fleischer and Frieda Zames, *The Disability Rights Movement: From Charity to Confrontation* (Philadelphia: Temple University Press, 2001); Joseph P. Shapiro, *No Pity: People with Disabilities Forging a New Civil Rights Movement* (New York: Times Books, 1993).

2. David L. Braddock and Susan L. Parish, "An Institutional History of Disability," in Gary L. Albrecht, Katherine D. Seelman, and Michael Bury (eds.), *Handbook of Disability Studies* (Thousand Oaks, CA: Sage, 2001).

3. Robert Bogdan, *Freak Show: Presenting Human Oddities for Amusement and Profit* (Chicago: University of Chicago Press, 1988).

4. Braddock and Parish, op. cit. Shapiro, op. cit.

5. Lennard J. Davis, "Why Disability Studies Matters" (retrieved from www.dpi.org/en/resources/articles/03-11-05_studies.htm, 2005).

6. Sanyika Shakur, *Monster: The Autobiography of an L.A. Gang Member* (New York: Penguin, 1993).

7. Colin Barnes and Geoff Mercer, "Disability Culture: Assimilation or Inclusion?" in Gary L. Albrecht, Katherine D. Seelman, and Michael Bury (eds.), *Handbook of Disability Studies* (Thousand Oaks, CA: Sage, 2001). Mark Deal, "Disabled People's Attitudes toward Other Impairment Groups: A Hierarchy of Impairments," *Disability and Society* 18 (2003), pp. 897–910. Margaret Carlisle Duncan, "The Sociology of Ability and Disability," *Sociology of Sport Journal* 18 (2001), pp.

1–4. John Hockenberry, *Moving Violations: War Zones, Wheelchairs, and Declarations of Independence* (New York: Hyperion, 1995). Marie Meyers and Brent Hardin, "The 'Supercrip' in Sport Media: Wheelchair Athletes Discuss Hegemony's Disabled Hero." *Sociology of Sport Online* 7(1) (retrieved from http://physed.otago. ac.nz/sosol/v7i1/v7il_1.html, 2004). Shapiro, op. cit. "Beez" Lea Ann Shell and Stephanie Rodriguez, "Subverting Bodies/Ambivalent Representations: Media Analysis of Paralympian, Hope Lewellen," *Sociology of Sport Journal* 18 (2001), pp. 127–135. Susan Wendell, *The Rejected Body: Feminist Philosophical Reflections on Disability* (New York: Routledge, 1996).

8. Ronald J. Berger, "Pushing Forward: Disability, Basketball, and Me," *Qualitative Inquiry* 10 (2004), pp. 794–810. Ronald J. Berger, "Hoop Dreams on Wheels," in Ronald J. Berger and Richard Quinney (eds.), *Storytelling Sociology: Narrative as Social Inquiry* (Boulder, CO: Lynne Rienner Publishers, 2005).

9. Jeffrey C. Alexander, *Action and Its Environments: Toward A New Synthesis* (New York: Columbia University Press, 1988). Jeffrey C. Alexander, *Positivism, Presuppositions, and Current Controversies* (Berkeley: University of California Press, 1982). Margaret S. Archer, *Culture and Agency: The Place of Culture in Social Theory* (Cambridge: Cambridge University Press, 1988). Mustafa Emirbayer and Ann Mische, "What is Agency?," *American Journal of Sociology* 103 (1998), pp. 962–1023. Anthony Giddens, *The Constitution of Society: Outline of the Theory of Structuration* (Berkeley: University of California Press, 1984). William H. Sewell, Jr., "A Theory of Structure: Duality, Agency, and Transformation," *American Journal of Sociology* 98 (1992), pp. 1–29.

10. James R. Grossman, Ann Durkin Keating, and Janice L. Reiff (eds.), *Encyclopedia of Chicago* (Chicago: University of Chicago Press, 2004). Cyril D. Robinson, "The Production of Black Violence in Chicago," in D. Greenberg (ed.), *Crime and Capitalism* (Philadelphia: Temple University Press, 1993). Steward E. Tolnay, Kyle D. Crowder, and Robert M. Adelman, "Race, Regional Origin, and Residence in Northern Cities at the Beginning of the Great Migration," *American Sociological Review* 67 (2002), pp. 456–475. Dempsey J. Travis, *An Autobiography of Black Chicago* (Chicago: Urban Research Institute, 1981).

11. Mary E. Pattillo, "Sweet Mothers and Gangbangers: Managing Crime in a Black Middle-Class Neighborhood," *Social Forces* 76 (1998), pp. 747–774. Robert J. Sampson and William Julius Wilson, "Race, Crime and Urban Inequality," in John Hagan and Ruth Peterson (eds.), *Crime and Inequality* (Stanford, CA: Stanford University Press, 1995). William Julius Wilson, *The Truly Disadvantaged: The Inner City, the Underclass, and Public Policy* (Chicago: University of Chicago Press, 1987).

12. Elijah Anderson, *Code of the Street: Decency, Violence, and the Moral Life of the Inner City* (New York: Norton, 1999).

13. Ruth Horowitz, "Community Tolerance of Gang Violence," *Social Problems* 34 (1987), pp. 432–450. Francis A. J. Ianni, "New Mafia: Black, Hispanic and Italian Styles," in Francis A. Ianni and Elizabeth Reuss-Ianni (eds.), *The Crime*

Society: Organized Crime and Corruption in America (New York: New American Library, 1976). Useni Eugene Perkins, Explosion of Chicago's Black Street Gangs: 1900 to the Present (Chicago: Third World Press, 1987). Robinson, op. cit. Randall G. Shelden, Sharon K. Tracy, and William B. Brown, Youth Gangs in American Society, 3rd ed. (Belmont, CA: Wadsworth, 2004). Frederick Thrasher, The Gang (Chicago: University of Chicago Press, 1927). Jerome H. Skolnick, "Gangs in the Post-Industrial Ghetto," The American Prospect 9 (Winter), 1992, pp. 109–120. Sudhir Alladi Venkatesh, "The Social Organization of Street Gang Activity in an Urban Ghetto," American Journal of Sociology 103 (1997), pp. 82–111.

14. Joan Moore, Diego Vigil, and Robert Garcia, "Residence and Territoriality in Chicano Gangs," Social Problems 31 (1983), pp. 182–194. Robert J. Sampson, "Transcending Tradition: New Directions in Community Research, Chicago Style," Criminology 40 (2002), pp. 213–230. Irving A. Spergel, "Youth Gangs; Continuity and Change," in Michael Tonry and Norval Morris (eds.), Crime and Justice: A Review of Research, Vol. 12 (Chicago: University of Chicago Press, 1990).

15. Sociologists in the symbolic interactionist tradition have been among the chief proponents of this position. See, for example, Kent L. Sandstrom, Daniel D. Martin, and Gary Alan Fine, Symbols, Selves and Social Reality: A Symbolic Interactionist Approach to Social Psychology and Sociology, 2nd ed. (Los Angeles: Roxbury, 2006).

16. Albert Bandura, Self-Efficacy: The Exercise of Control (New York: W. H. Freeman, 1997). Viktor Gecas, "The Social Psychology of Self-Efficacy," Annual Review of Sociology 15 (1989), pp. 291–316. Viktor Gecas and Michael L. Schwalbe, "Beyond the Looking Glass Self: Social Structure and Efficacy-Based Self-Esteem," Social Psychology Quarterly 46 (1983), pp. 77–88. James E. Maddux (ed.), Self-Efficacy, Adaptation, and Adjustment: Theory, Research, and Application (New York: Plenum, 1995). Sandstrom et al., op. cit.

17. Emirbayer and Mische, op. cit.

18. David Dawley, A Nation of Lords: The Autobiography of the Vice Lords (Prospect Heights, IL: Waveland Press, 1992). Shakur, op. cit. James W. Messerschmidt, Nine Lives: Adolescent Masculinities, Bodies, and Violence (Boulder, CO: Westview Press, 2000).

19. Norman K. Denzin, Interpretive Biography (Newbury Park, CA: Sage, 1989).

20. Ibid., quote on p. 70.

21. Arthur W. Frank, "The Rhetoric of Self-Change: Illness Experience as Narrative," Sociological Quarterly 34 (1993), pp. 39–52, quote on p. 42.

22. Murphy was the first to apply this concept to disability: See Robert Murphy, The Body Silent (New York: Henry Holt, 1987), and Robert Murphy, Jessica Scheer, Yolanda Murphy, and Robert Mack, "Physical Disability and Social Liminality: A Study in the Rituals of Adversity," Social Science and Medicine 26 (1988), pp. 235–242. Earlier, Arnold van Gennep and Victor Turner applied this concept to cultural rites of passage: See Arnold van Gennep, The Rites of Passage

(Chicago: University of Chicago Press, [1909] 1960), and Victor Turner, "Betwixt and Between: The Liminal Period in *Rites de Passage,"* in William Lessa and Evon Vogt (eds.), *Reader in Contemporary Religion,* 4th ed. (New York: Harper and Row, [1964] 1979).

23. Patrick Sharkey defines *street efficacy* as the "perceived ability to avoid violent confrontations and to be safe in one's neighborhood." But his empirical support for the proposition that street efficacy is inversely related to violence is based on a tautology: He operationalizes efficacy as persons' *perceived* ability to avoid violence, which, not surprisingly, is statistically associated with persons' *actual* ability to avoid violence. See Patrick T. Sharkey, "Navigating Dangerous Streets: The Sources and Consequences of Street Efficacy," *American Sociological Review* 71 (2006), pp. 826–846, quote on p. 826.

My view of Melvin's street efficacy is more in line with Douglas Massey's conception of violence as a rational strategy for negotiating public life on the streets. That Melvin ultimately fell victim to street violence does not negate a characterization of him as an efficacious agent of his environment. See Douglas S. Massey, "Getting Away with Murder: Segregation and Violent Crime in Urban America," *Pennsylvania Law Review* 143 (1995), pp. 1203–1232.

24. R. W. Connell, *Masculinities* (Berkeley: University of California Press 1995). Thomas J. Gerschick and Adam S. Miller, "Coming to Terms: Masculinity and Physical Disability," in Donald Sabo and David Frederick Gordon (eds.), *Men's Health and Illness: Gender, Power and the Body* (Thousand Oaks, CA: Sage, 1995). Brett Smith and Andrew S. Sparkes, "Men, Sport, and Spinal Cord Injury: An Analysis of Metaphors and Narrative Types," *Disability and Society* 19 (2004), pp. 613–626.

25. Chris Shilling, *The Body and Social Theory* (Thousand Oaks, CA: Sage, 2003), quote on p. 113. See also James W. Messerschmidt, *Flesh and Blood: Adolescent Gender Diversity and Violence* (Lanham, MD: Rowman & Littlefield, 2004).

26. Frank, op. cit.

27. See Jane Mansbridge and Aldon D. Morris (eds.), *Oppositional Consciousness: The Subjective Roots of Protest* (Chicago: University of Chicago Press, 2001).

28. Fleischer and Zames, op. cit. Mike Oliver, *The Politics of Disablement* (Basingstoke, Great Britain: Macmillan, 1990). Andrew Potok, *A Matter of Dignity: Changing the World of the Disabled* (New York: Bantam Books, 2002). Richard K. Scotch, *From Good Will to Civil Rights: Transforming Federal Disability Policy* (Philadelphia: Temple University Press, 2001). Shapiro, op cit. Claire Tregasis, "Social Model Theory: The Story So Far . . ." *Disability and Society* 17 (2002), pp. 457–470.

29. Michelle Fine and Adrienne Asch, "Disability Beyond Stigma; Social Interaction, Discrimination, and Activism," *Journal of Social Issues* 44 (1988), pp. 3–21, quote on p. 11.

30. Joseph M. Camilleri, "Disability: A Personal Odyssey," *Disability and Society* 14 (1999), pp. 845–853. Carol J. Gill, "Divided Understandings: The Social

Experience of Disability," in Gary L. Albrecht, Katherine D. Seelman, and Michael Bury (eds.), *Handbook of Disability Studies* (Thousand Oaks, CA: Sage, 2001). Richard K. Scotch, "Disability as the Basis for a Social Movement: Advocacy and the Politics of Definition," *Journal of Social Issues* 44 (1988), pp. 159–172. Randy Snow, *Pushing Forward: A Memoir of Motivation* (Dubuque, IA: Kendall/Hunt, 2001). Beatrice Wright, *Physical Disability: A Psychosocial Approach* (New York: Harper & Row, 1960).

31. Barnes and Mercer, op. cit. Leonard J. Davis, "Identity Politics, Disability, and Culture," in Gary L. Albrecht, Katherine D. Seelman, and Michael Bury (eds.), *Handbook of Disability Studies* (Thousand Oaks, CA: Sage, 2001). Deal, op. cit. David M. Engel and Frank W. Munger, *Rights of Inclusion: Law and Identity in the Life Stories of Americans with Disabilities* (Chicago: University of Chicago Press, 2003). Rose Galvin, "The Paradox of Disability Culture: The Need to Combine versus the Imperative to Let Go," *Disability and Society* 18 (2003), pp. 675–690. Stephen French Gilson and Elizabeth Depoy, "Multiculturalism and Disability: A Critical Perspective," *Disability and Society* 15 (2000), pp. 207–217. Beth Omansky Gordon and Karen E. Rosenblum, "Bringing Disability into the Sociological Frame: A Comparison of Disability with Race, Sex, and Sexual Orientation Statuses," *Disability and Society* 16 (2001), pp. 5–19. Ayesha Vernon, "The Dialectics of Multiple Identities and the Disabled People's Movement," *Disability and Society* 14 (1999), pp. 385–398. Wendell, op. cit.

32. Deal, op. cit. Engel and Munger, op. cit. Ruth Galvin, "The Making of the Disabled Identity: A Linguistic Analysis of Marginalisation," *Disability and Society* 23 (2003), pp. 149–178. Nick Watson, "Well, I Know This Is Going to Sound Very Strange to You, but I Don't See Myself as a Disabled Person: Identity and Disability," *Disability and Society* 17 (2002), pp. 509–527.

33. Engel and Munger, op. cit., p. 14.

34. Cheryl L. Cole, "Body Studies in the Sociology of Sport," in Jay Coakley and Eric Dunning (eds.), *Handbook of Sports Studies* (Thousand Oaks, CA: Sage, 2002). David Promis, Nirmala Erevelles, and Jerry Matthews, "Reconceptualizing Inclusion: The Politics of University Sports and Recreation Programs for Students with Mobility Impairments," *Sociology of Sport Journal* 18 (2001), pp. 37–50.

35. Promis et al., op. cit., quote on p. 39.

36. Michael Schwalbe and Douglas Mason-Schrock, "Identity Work as Group Process," *Advances in Group Process* 13 (1996), pp. 113–147, quote on p. 141. See also David A. Snow and Leon Anderson, "Identity Work among the Homeless: The Verbal Construction and Avowal of Personal Identities," *American Journal of Sociology* 92 (1987), pp. 1336–1371.

37. Karen P. DePauw and Susan J. Gavron, *Disability and Sport* (Champaign, IL: Human Kinetics, 1995). Brad Hedrick, Dan Byrnes, and Lew Shaver, *Wheelchair Basketball*, 2nd ed. (Washington, DC: Paralyzed Veterans of America, 1994). National Wheelchair Basketball Association (NWBA), "History of Wheelchair Basketball" (retrieved from www.nwba.org/history.html, 2004). Ralph W. Smith,

David R. Austin, Dan W. Kennedy, Youngkhill Lee, and Peggy Hutchison, *Inclusive and Special Recreation: Opportunities for Persons with Disabilities,* 5th ed. (New York: McGraw-Hill, 2005).

38. Jay Coakley, *Sports in Society: Issues and Controversies,* 4th ed. (Boston: McGraw-Hill).

39. Varda Burstyn, *The Rites of Men: Manhood, Politics, and the Culture of Sport* (Toronto: University of Toronto Press, 1999). James McKay, Michael A. Messner, and David Sabo, *Masculinities, Gender Relations, and Sport* (Newbury Park, CA: Sage, 2000). Michael A. Messner, *Power at Play: Sports and the Problem of Masculinity* (Boston: Beacon Press, 1992). William Pollack, *Real Boys: Rescuing Our Sons from the Myth of Boyhood* (New York: Henry Holt, 1998). Nancy Therberg, "Gender and Sport," in Jay Coakley and Eric Dunning (eds.), *Handbook of Sports Studies* (Thousand Oaks, CA: Sage, 2002).

40. Harland Hahn, "Sports and the Political Movement of Disabled Persons: Examining Nondisabled Social Values." *Arena Review* 8 (1984), pp.1–15. Howard L. Nixon II, "Sport and Disability," in Jay Coakley and Eric Dunning (eds.), *Handbook of Sports Studies* (Thousand Oaks, CA: Sage, 2002).

41. Candace Ashton-Shaeffer, Heather J. Gibson, Cari E. Autry, and Carolyn S. Hanson, "Meaning of Sport to Adults with Physical Disabilities: A Disability Sport Camp Experience," *Sociology of Sport Journal* 18 (2001), pp. 95–114. Bob Baird, "Altered State," *Sports 'N Spokes,* January (2005), pp. 48–51. Elaine M. Blinde and Lisa R. McClung, "Enhancing the Physical and Social Self through Recreational Activity: Accounts of Individuals with Physical Disabilities," *Adapted Physical Activity Quarterly* 14 (1997), pp. 327–344. Frank M. Brasile and Brad N. Hedrick, "A Comparison of Participation Incentives Between Adult and Youth Wheelchair Basketball Players," *Palaestra: The Forum of Sport, Physical Education and Recreation for the Disabled* 7 (1991), pp. 40–46. Frank M. Brasile, Douglas A. Kleiber, and Delwin Harnisch, "Analysis of Participation Incentives Among Athletes With and Without Disabilities," *Therapeutic Recreation Journal* 25 (1991), pp. 18–33. C. Michael Greenwood, David A. Dzewaltowski, and Ron French, "Self-Efficacy and Psychological Well-Being of Wheelchair Tennis Participants and Wheelchair Nontennis Participants," *Adapted Physical Activity Quarterly* 7 (1990), pp. 12–21. Sharon R. Guthrie and Shirley Castelnuovo, "Disability Management among Women with Physical Impairments: The Contribution of Physical Activity." *Sociology of Sport Journal* 18 (2001), pp. 5–20. Bradley Noble Hedrick, "Wheelchair Sports as a Mechanism for Altering the Perceptions of the Nondisabled Regarding Their Disabled Peers' Competence," *Therapeutic Recreation Journal* 20 (1986), pp. 72–84. Keith P. Henschen, Michale Horvat, and Glenn Roswal. "Psychological Profiles of the United States Wheelchair Basketball Team," *International Journal of Sport Psychology* 23 (1992), pp. 128–137. Chris Hopper and James Santomier, "Self Esteem and Aspirations of Wheelchair Athletes," *Humboldt Journal of Social Relations* 12 (1984), pp. 24–35. Patricia Paulsen, Ron French, and Claudine Sherill. "Comparison of Wheelchair Athletes and Nonathletes on Selected Mood States,"

Perceptual and Motor Skills 71 (1990), pp. 1160–1162. Lew Shaver, *Damn Bunch of Cripples: My Politically Incorrect Education in Disability Awareness* (New York: iUniverse, 2003). Diane E. Taub, Elaine M. Blinde, and Kimberly R. Greer, "Stigma Management through Participation in Sport and Physical Activity: Experiences of Male College Students with Physical Disabilities," *Human Relations* 52 (1999), pp. 1469–1484. Pamela E. Wilson, "Exercise and Sports for Children Who Have Disabilities," *Physical Medicine and Rehabilitation Clinics of North America* 13 (2002), pp. 907–923. Sally A. White and Joan L. Duda, "Dimensions of Goals and Beliefs Among Adolescent Athletes with Disabilities," *Adapted Physical Activity Quarterly* 10 (1993), pp. 125–136.

42. Elaine M. Blinde, Diane E. Taub, and Lingling Han, "Sport Participation and Women's Personal Empowerment: Experiences of the College Athlete," in Andrew Yiannakis and Merrill J. Melnick (eds.), *Contemporary Issues in Sociology of Sport* (Champaign, IL: Human Kinetics, 2001), quote on p. 163.

43. Ann Goetting, "Fictions of the Self," in Ann Goetting and Sarah Fenstermaker (eds.), *Individual Voices, Collective Visions: Fifty Years of Women in Sociology* (Philadelphia: Temple University Press, 1995).

44. See Denzin, op. cit., pp. 47–48, for definitions of the various forms in this genre. Generally, the life-story method is noted for telling the story in the person's own words. See Robert Atkinson, *The Life Story Interview* (Thousand Oaks, CA: Sage, 1998).

45. C. Wright Mills, *The Sociological Imagination* (New York: Oxford University Press, 1959).

46. Denzin, op. cit. Goetting, op. cit., quote on p. 7. Messerschmidt, op. cit., 2004.

47. Norman K. Denzin, "Interpretive Ethnography for the Next Century," *Journal of Contemporary Ethnography* 28 (1999), pp. 510–519. George C. Rosenwald and Richard L. Ochberg (eds.), *Storied Lives: The Cultural Politics of Self-Understanding* (New Haven, CT: Yale University Press), quote on p. 7.

48. Jaber F. Gubrium and James A. Holstein, "At the Border of Narrative and Ethnography," *Journal of Contemporary Ethnography* 28 (1999), pp. 561–573, quote on pp. 569–570. Rosenwald and Ochberg, op. cit.

49. Ronald J. Berger and Richard Quinney (eds.), *Storytelling Sociology: Narrative as Social Inquiry* (Boulder, CO: Lynne Rienner Publishers, 2005). Norman K. Denzin, *Interpretive Ethnography: Ethnographic Practices for the Twenty-first Century* (Thousand Oaks, CA: Sage, 1997). Denzin (1989), op. cit.

50. Gill, op. cit.

51. Goetting, op. cit.

52. Atkinson, op. cit. Berger and Quinney, op. cit. Denzin (1999), op. cit. Duncan, op. cit. Michael Jackson, *Minima Ethnographica: Intersubjectivity and the Anthropological Project* (Chicago: Chicago University Press, 1998). Daniel Taylor, *Tell Me a Story: The Life-Shaping Power of Stories* (St. Paul, MN: Bog Walk, 2001).

53. Atkinson, op. cit. Goetting, op. cit., quote on p. 15.

54. Ingeborg K. Helling calls this the "narrative-interview" approach; see "The Life History Method: A Survey and Discussion with Norman K. Denzin," in Norman K. Denzin (ed.), *Studies in Symbolic Interaction,* Vol. 12 (Greenwich, CT: JAI Press, 1988).

55. Denzin (1989), op. cit. Goetting, op. cit. Robert McKee, *Story: Substance, Structure, Style, and the Principles of Screenwriting* (New York: ReganBooks, 1997). Francesca Polletta and John Lee, "Is Telling Stories Good for Democracy? Rhetoric in Public Deliberation after 9/11," *American Sociological Review* 71 (2006), pp. 699–723.

56. Arthur W. Frank, *The Wounded Storyteller: Body, Illness, and Ethics* (Chicago: University of Chicago Press, 1995), quotes on pp. 133 and 171. William F. May, *The Patient's Ordeal* (Bloomington: Indiana University Press, 1991). Smith and Sparkes, op. cit.

57. John Barth, *Lost in the Funhouse: Fiction for Print, Tape, Live Voice* (New York: Doubleday, 1968), quote on p. 96.

58. Goetting, op. cit., quote on p. 13.

59. Atkinson, op. cit., quote on p. 60.

60. Goetting, op. cit. Georges Gusdorf, "Conditions and Limits of Autobiography," in James Olney (ed.), *Autobiography: Essays Theoretical and Critical* (Princeton, NJ: Princeton University Press, 1980). James Young, *Writing and Rewriting the Holocaust* (Indianapolis: Indiana University Press, 1988).

61. Denzin (1989), op. cit., quote on p. 83.

62. Atkinson, op. cit., quote on p. 20.

63. Elisabeth Kübler-Ross, *On Death and Dying* (New York: Scribner, 1967). Although Kübler-Ross developed her scheme to account for the process of grieving over death, it is often applied to disability as well. See Hockenberry, op. cit.

64. Michel Foucault, "Technologies of the Self," in Luther H. Martin, Huck Gutman, and Patrick H. Hutton (eds.), *Technologies of the Self: A Seminar with Michel Foucault* (Amherst: University of Massachusetts Press, 1988).

65. Hockenberry, op. cit., quote on pp. 79, 86.

1. Roots

1. Grossman et al., op. cit.

2. Jeff Todd Titon and Alan Trachtenberg, *Early Downhome Blues: A Musical and Cultural Analysis* (Chapel Hill: University of North Carolina Press, 1995).

2. In the Company of Peers

1. For discussions of this demeanor, see Richard Majors and Janet Mancini Billson, *Cool Pose: The Dilemmas of Black Manhood in America* (New York: Lexington Books, 1992) and Nathan McCall, *Makes Me Wanna Holler: A Young Black Man in America* (New York: Vintage, 1994).

2. Melvin and his friends variously called these teasing/insult routines jonin', capin', bustin' on people, or simply trash-talking. Historically they were called "playing the dozens." Speculation has it that "playing the dozens" originated among field slaves who used verbal insults to express their resentment toward the more privileged (and often lighter skinned) black house workers. The term *dozens* may have referred to the claim that an adversary's mother was one of dozens of women who were sexually available to the master. See Majors and Billson, op. cit.

3. Gangs

1. See David Matza, *Delinquency and Drift* (New York: John Wiley and Sons, 1967).

2. Carolyn Rebecca Block and Richard Block, "Street Gang Crime in Chicago," *National Institute of Justice: Research in Brief* (Washington, DC: U.S. Department of Justice, December 1993). Chicago Police Department, unpublished mimeograph, n.d. Florida Department of Corrections, "Street Gangs–Chicago Based or Influenced" (retrieved from www.dc.state.fl.us/pub/gangs/chicago.html, 2002). John Hagedorn, *People and Folks: Gangs, Crime and the Underclass in a Rustbelt City* (Chicago: Lake View Press, 1987). John Irwin, *Prisons in Turmoil* (Boston: Little, Brown, 1980). James B. Jacobs, *Stateville: The Penitentiary in Mass Society* (Chicago: University of Chicago Press, 1977). Madison Police Department, "People and Folks" (retrieved from www.ci.madison.wi.us/police/pf.html, 2002). Perkins, op. cit. Robinson, op. cit. Lance Williams, "The Almighty Black P Stone Nation: Black Power, Politics, and Gangbanging" (retrieved from www.gangresearch.net/ChicagoGangs/blackstonerangers/lance.htm, 2006).

5. Road to Recovery

1. DePauw and Gavron, op. cit. Hedrick et al., op. cit. Brad Hedrick and Sharon Hedrick, "Women's Wheelchair Basketball," in Joan S. Hult and Marianna Trekell (eds.), *A Century of Women's Basketball: From Frailty to Final Four* (Reston, VA: American Alliance for Health, Physical Education, Recreation and Dance, 1991). Stan Labanowich, "The Physically Disabled in Sports," *Sports 'N Spokes* reprint, March–April (1987), pp. 1–6. Stan Labanowich, "Wheelchair Basketball Classification: National and International Perspectives," *PALAESTRA: The Forum of Sport, Physical Education and Recreation for the Disabled,* Spring (1988), pp. 14–15, 38–40, 54. NWBA, op. cit. Smith et al., op. cit.

2. The first national women's tournament was held in 1975.

3. "NWBA Bylaws" (retrieved from www.nwba.org/bylaws.html, 2005).

4. Thomas John LaMere and Stan Labanowich, "The History of Sport Wheelchairs—Part I: The Development of the Basketball Wheelchair," *Sports 'N Spokes* reprint, March–April (1984), pp. 1–4. Shapiro, op. cit.

5. Today, several manufacturers design lightweight sports chairs for use in a variety of athletic venues. See advertisements in *Sports 'N Spokes*, published by the Paralyzed Veterans of America, 2111 East Highland Avenue, Suite 180, Phoenix, AZ 85016.

6. Snow, op. cit., quote on p. 38.

6. Breaking Away

1. We thank John Truesdale for his help compiling this background on the UWW program. See National Association of Student Personnel Administrators, *Bridges to Student Success: Exemplary Programs* (Washington, DC: NASPA, 1999).

2. See Hedrick et al., op. cit.

7. A Motley Crew

1. We thank Mike Frogley for sharing this account.

2. We thank Eric Barber for sharing this account.

3. Frank M. Brasile, "Performance Evaluation of Wheelchair Athletes: More than a Disability Classification Level Issue," *Adapted Physical Activity Quarterly* 7 (1990), pp. 289–297. Nancy Crase, "Rules and Regs: How Wheelchair Basketball Is Played," *Sports 'N Spokes* reprint, May–June (1982). Labanowich (1988), op. cit., quote on p. 14.

4. In 2006–2007 the NWBA began experimenting with a four-point classification scheme for its Division I and collegiate divisions that is similar to the international system.

5. "International Paralympic Committee" (retrieved from www.paralympic.org/release/Main_Sections_Menu/index.html, 2005). "International Wheelchair Basketball Federation" (retrieved from www.iwbf.org/onder.htm, 2005). Labanowich (1987), op. cit. Nixon, op. cit. Smith et al., op. cit. The first Paralympic winter games were held in Sweden in 1976.

6. In 1957, under the leadership of Benjamin Lipton, the coach of the Bulova Watchmakers, a New York team sponsored by the Bulova Watch Company, the United States hosted its first multievent National Wheelchair Games. From this emerged the National Wheelchair Athletic Association, later called Wheelchair Sports USA (WSUSA), which facilitates U.S. participation in international competition. In 1993, the NWBA affiliated with WSUSA and is currently the governing body for the selection, training, and fielding of U.S. teams that compete in international basketball competition. At the international level, the International Paralympic Committee coordinates the Paralympics and the International Wheelchair Basketball Federation coordinates the Gold Cup.

Paralympic athletes and coaches are sometimes disgruntled that the Special Olympics gets more publicity and that the public often confuses these two sport competitions. They also question the persistent segregation of wheelchair basketball from the regular Olympics. Brad Hedrick, for example, wonders why the International Olympic Committee (IOC) fast-tracked beach volleyball and mountain-bike racing from recreational pursuits to Olympic status in 1996 while they continued to deem a sport like wheelchair basketball less legitimate, less deserving of such inclusion. Is it because athletes with disabilities are not really athletes after all? Why not instead view the wheelchair as a piece of equipment and allow able-bodied people to play, giving them the highest classification, as is done in Canada under Canadian Wheelchair Basketball Association rules. (For all practical purposes, there is no difference between a NWBA Class III or Paralympic 4.5 disabled player and an able-bodied player. Both have full upper-body function that enables them to shoot and rebound, pass and catch, and bend over and pick up a ball; they both can use their abs, trunk, and hip flexors for stability, speed, and balance.) Thus, Hedrick asks, "Why is there no clearly defined process by which eligible sports for athletes with disabilities could be incorporated into the more inclusive context of the Olympic movement?" Why does the IOC continue to preserve the "complete programmatic separation" of athletes with disabilities from athletes without disabilities? Apparently, the IOC does not mind "if athletes with disabilities get on the bus, as long as they sit in the back" of the bus. See Brad Hedrick, "Olympic Inequities," *Sports 'N Spokes,* November (2000), p. 74.

8. Fundamentally Sound

1. Chungliang Al Huang and Jerry Lynch, *Thinking Body, Dancing Mind: Tao-Sports for Extraordinary Performance in Athletics, Business, and Life* (New York: Bantam, 1992), quotes on pp. 10–11.

2. See Hedrick et al., op. cit.

3. See Shaver, op. cit.

4. Tip Thiboutot, "Panning for Gold," *Sports 'N Spokes,* September/October (1994), pp. 25–27.

5. Elaine Bliah, "Red, White, and Blue," *Sports 'N Spokes,* September (2003), pp. 46–50.

6. Robert J. Szyman, "Four on the Floor," *Sports 'N Spokes,* May/June (1996), pp. 48–50.

7. Hagedorn, op. cit. Linda Stoneall, "Rural Gang Origins: A Wisconsin Case Study," *Sociological Imagination* 34 (1997), pp. 45–58.

8. Marvin D. Free, Jr., *African Americans and the Criminal Justice System* (New York: Garland, 1996). Marvin D. Free, Jr. (ed.), *Racial Issues in Criminal Justice: The Case of African Americans* (New York: Praeger, 2004). Darrell Steffensmeier, Jeffery Ulmer, and John Kramer, "The Interaction of Race, Gender, and Age in Criminal Sentencing: The Punishment Cost of Being Young, Black, and Male," *Criminology* 36 (1998), pp. 763–798.

9. It is not uncommon for black women to resent black men who marry white women because they view it as depleting the supply of available black partners.

More generally, some African Americans disapprove of interracial marriages because of concern that the offspring of such marriages will not perpetuate the race. See Patricia H. Collins, *Black Feminist Thought* (New York: Routledge, 1990); Kellina M. Craig-Henderson, *Black Men in Interracial Relationships: What's Love Got to Do with It?* (New Brunswick, NJ: Transaction, 2006); Paul. C. Rosenblatt, Terri A. Karis, and Richard D. Powell, *Multiracial Couples: Black and White Voices* (Thousand Oaks, CA: Sage, 1995); Paul R. Spickard, *Mixed Blood: Intermarriage and Ethnic Identity in Twentieth-Century America* (Madison: University of Wisconsin Press, 1989); and Robert Staples and Leanor Boulin Johnson, *Black Families at the Crossroads: Challenges and Prospects* (San Francisco: Jossey-Bass, 1993).

10. On average, biracial couples do experience more marital stress from unsupportive family members than do same-race couples. See Ann Y. Chan and Ken R. Smith, "Perceived Marital Quality and Stability of Intermarried Couples: A Study of Asian-White, Black-White, and Mexican-White Couples," *Sociological Imagination* 37 (2000), pp. 230–256; Richard Lewis, Jr., and George Yancey, "Biracial Marriages in the United States: An Analysis of Variation in Family Member Support," *Sociological Spectrum* 41 (1995), pp. 443–462; and Rosenblatt, op. cit. On the stress of playing wheelchair basketball, see Elizabeth Campbell and Graham Jones, "Sources of Stress Experienced by Elite Male Wheelchair Basketball Players," *Adapted Physical Activity Quarterly* 19 (2002), pp. 82–89.

9. Lost and Found

1. We thank Mike Frogley and Jeremy Lade for sharing this account.

2. Currently the camp also offers sledge hockey, water skiing, rope climbing, and horseback riding.

3. Maurice was on house arrest and could not attend the games.

4. Jim Gallo, "All That Glitters Is Not Gold," *Sports 'N Spokes,* Special Commemorative Issue, October (1996), pp. 41–43.

5. *Sports 'N Spokes,* "X Paralympic Games," Special Commemorative Issue, October (1996).

6. Gallo, op. cit., quotes on p. 43. Tip Thiboutot, "U.S.A. Basketball: The Humility Gap," *Sports 'N Spokes,* Special Commemorative Issue, October (1996), pp. 45–47.

7. Gallo, op. cit., quote on p. 43.

8. Ibid.

9. Campbell and Jones, op. cit.

10. Al Huang and Lynch, op. cit., quotes on p. 11.

11. That Melvin married two white women raised the ire of one of our reviewers, who rather remarkably accused him of self-hatred for rejecting his blackness and conspicuously avoiding black women. This attribution misreads limited research that has uncovered a disposition among some black men to avoid

black women (Craig-Henderson, op. cit.) and ignores a larger body of research that finds that most people become involved in interracial relationships for the same reasons they become involved in intraracial relationships, because of "love, companionship, compatibility, and other positive aspects of relationship that anyone might want. . . . [P]eople who were drawn to each other connected as people, not categories" (Rosenblatt et al., op. cit., pp. 39, 250; Maria P. Root, *Love's Revolution: Interracial Marriage* [Philadelphia: Temple University Press, 2001]; Barbara Tizard, *Black, White or Mixed Race? Race and Racism in the Lives of Young People of Mixed Parentage* [New York: Routledge, 2002]). It is no doubt true that some African Americans disapprove of interracial relationships, as do some whites (see Chapter 8, note 9 above). But the relative size of the black and white populations in a person's immediate milieu is a more likely factor affecting the selection of partners than intentional avoidance based on race (Rosenblatt, op. cit.; Spickard, op. cit; Staples and Johnson, op. cit.). In Melvin's case, his decision to remain in Whitewater limited his chances of meeting black women. He has felt no obligation to move back to Chicago or avoid involvement with white women merely because some people may have a problem with his decisions. Moreover, research shows that African Americans who marry interracially are no less likely than those who marry intraracially to think positively of their black identity (Rosenblatt, op. cit.). It is perhaps regrettable that in the guise of critical analysis of race, some "politically correct" sociologists end up reinforcing the solidity of categories they ostensibly seek to challenge.

10. The Best of All Victories

1. Tip Thiboutot, "Bringing Home the Medals," *Sports 'N Spokes,* January (1999), pp. 40–43.

2. Ibid., quote on p. 40.

3. Tip Thiboutot, "The Fire Within: Paralympics," *Sports 'N Spokes,* December (2000), pp. 38–57.

4. Jim Gallo, "Accepting the Torch," *Sports 'N Spokes,* May (2003), pp. 9–11.

5. Tip Thiboutot, "Global Roundball," *Sports 'N Spokes,* June (2002), pp. 8–15, quote on p. 12.

6. Ibid., quote on p. 14.

7. Tip Thiboutot, "Chasing Gold," *Sports 'N Spokes,* November (2002), pp. 22–27, quote on p. 25.

8. *Sports 'N Spokes,* "Major Hoop-La," May (2003), pp. 37–55.

9. *Sports 'N Spokes,* "Spirit of Performance," November (2004), pp. 38–62, quote on pp. 40–41.

10. The U.S. women's basketball team, coached by Ron Lykins, did win a gold medal.

11. Snow, op. cit., quote on p. 138.

Conclusion

1. William Ryan, *Blaming the Victim* (New York: Vintage, 1971).

2. See Introduction, note 9.

3. Engel and Munger, op. cit.

4. Gecas, op. cit.

5. Anderson, op. cit.

6. See Introduction, note 24.

7. Engel and Munger, op. cit., quote on p. 103.

8. See Introduction, note 28.

9. John H. Laub, Daniel S. Nagin, and Robert J. Sampson, "Trajectories of Change in Criminal Offending: Good Marriages and the Desistance Process," *American Sociological Review* 63 (1998), pp. 225–238. Robert J. Sampson and John H. Laub, *Crime in the Making: Pathways and Turning Points through Life* (Cambridge, MA: Harvard University Press, 1993). Robert J. Sampson and John H. Laub, "Life-Course Desisters? Trajectories of Crime among Delinquent Boys Followed to Age 70." *Criminology* 41 (2003), pp. 555–592. Mark Warr, "Life-Course Transitions and Desistance from Crime," *Criminology* 36 (1998), pp. 183–216.

10. Frank (1995), op. cit.

11. Ibid.

12. Ibid., quote on p. 135.

13. Taylor, op. cit., quote on p. 75.

14. Frank, op. cit., quote on p. xi.

15. Bruce A. Arrigio (ed.), *Social Justice/Criminal Justice: The Maturation of Critical Theory in Law, Crime, and Deviance* (Belmont, CA: Wadsworth, 1999). Stuart Henry and Dragon Milovanovic, *Constitutive Criminology: Beyond Postmodernism* (London: Sage, 1996).

16. See Introduction, note 32.

17. Sandstrom et al., op. cit.

18. Engel and Munger, op. cit., quote on p. 46.

19. Kenneth Gergen, *The Saturated Self: Dilemmas of Identity in Contemporary Life* (New York: Basic Books, 1991).

20. Jaber Gubrium and James A. Holstein, "The Self in a World of Going Concerns," *Symbolic Interaction* 23 (2003), pp, 95–115, quote on p. 96.

21. Louis Zurcher, *The Mutable Self* (Beverly Hills, CA: Sage, 1977).

22. John Hewitt, *Self and Society,* 8th ed. (Boston: Allyn and Bacon, 2000). Sandstrom, op. cit., quote on p. 115.

23. Søren Kierkegaard, *Either/Or, Part II,* ed. and trans. Howard. V. Hong and Edna H. Hong (Princeton: Princeton University Press, 1987), quote on p. 260. Cited by Frank (1995), op. cit., p. xii.

24. Frank (1995), op. cit., quote on p. xiii.

25. We thank Mike Frogley for this observation.

26. Huang and Lynch, op. cit.

27. Snow, op. cit.

28. Frank (1993), op. cit.

29. Foucault, op. cit.

30. Frank (1993), op. cit., quote on p. 49.

31. See Introduction, note 36.

32. Frank (1993), op. cit.

33. David O. Friedrichs, "Postmodernism, Postmodernity, and Postmodern Criminology," in J. Fuller and E. Hickey (eds.), *Controversial Issues in Criminology* (Boston: Allyn and Bacon, 1999).

34. A. Manette Ansay, *Limbo: A Memoir* (New York: HarperCollins, 2001), quote on p. 265.

35. Having the opportunity to know Melvin and the other athletes I've met through my research on wheelchair basketball has fortified me in my own journey helping my daughter live with cerebral palsy. Throughout her life she has worked so very hard to maximize her potential, doing her strengthening and conditioning exercises, going through surgeries and other medical treatments. In many respects, she sometimes seems to me an athlete in training, and my wife and I seem not only her parents but her coaches and personal trainers. My daughter, thirteen years old at the time of this writing, objects to this analogy. "I don't want coaches," she says, "I want parents." She is wise beyond her years, but her dispute with my comparisons has not deterred me from thinking this way. See Berger (2004 and 2005), op. cit.

36. James Naismith, *Basketball: Its Origins and Development,* with Introduction by William Joseph Baker (Lincoln: University of Nebraska Press, [1941] 1996).

37. John Edgar Wideman, *Hoop Roots: Playground Basketball, Love, and Race* (Boston: Houghton Mifflin, 2001).

38. Dennis Trudell (ed.), *Full Court: A Literary Anthology of Basketball* (New York: Breakaway Books, 1996), quote on pp. 8–9.

39. Wideman, op. cit., quotes on pp. 1, 6, 7, 97, and 164.

40. Trudell, op. cit.

41. Wideman, op. cit., quote on p. 9.

42. Ibid., quotes on pp. 6 and 9.

43. Ibid., quote on p. 17.

Index

Melvin Juette is Community Service Coordinator of the Deferred Prosecution Unit of the Dane County District Attorney's Office in Madison, Wisconsin.

Ronald J. Berger is Professor of Sociology and Chair of the Department of Sociology, Anthropology, and Criminal Justice at the University of Wisconsin–Whitewater.

DATE DUE

JUN 1 0 2009			
JUL 0 1 2009			